CW00925684

Against All Odds

In memory of Kurt's parents

ALFRED and FRIEDA PICK

and of

MICHEL MATTON

EUGENE COUGNET

JULES PIETTE

and with grateful thanks to

MARIE-THERESE TOCK-MALAISE

and all those Belgians who risked their lives

sheltering Jews during the Holocaust

AGAINST ALL ODDS

The Story of Kurt Pick

Jennifer Henderson

THE RADCLIFFE PRESS
LONDON • NEW YORK

Published in 1998 by The Radcliffe Press
Victoria House, Bloomsbury Square
London WC1B 4DZ

In the United States and Canada
distributed by St. Martin's Press
175 Fifth Avenue, New York NY 10010

Copyright © Jennifer Henderson, 1998

All rights reserved. Except for brief quotations in a review, this book, or
any part thereof, may not be reproduced, stored in or introduced into a
retrieval system, or transmitted, in any form or by any means, electronic,
mechanical, photocopying, recording or otherwise, without the prior
written permission of the publisher.

ISBN 1 86064 252 7

A full CIP record for this book is available from the British Library
A full CIP record for this book is available from the Library of Congress

Library of Congress catalog card: available

Typeset in Garamond by Dexter Haven, London
Printed in Great Britain by WBC Ltd, Bridgend, Mid Glamorgan

Contents

Foreword   vii

Introduction   ix

PART I   BRUSSELS   1

   1   December 1938   3

   2   December 1938-June 1939   21

                    ❖

PART II   MARNEFFE AND BRUSSELS   49

   3   June 1939-May 1940   51

   4   May-June 1940   75

   5   June 1940-July 1942   95

                    ❖

PART III   BASSINES AND LIEGE   125

   6   July 1942-October 1943   127

   7   October 1943-September 1944   160

                    ❖

Epilogue   194

Some of the People in the Book   200

Index   202

Foreword

Anger and appreciation: these are the two feelings that tumble out side by side when I think of the extraordinary story of Kurt Pick. Anger that such a caring and creative person should have been discriminated against and persecuted by the homeland that should have valued him. Appreciation that his remarkable talents were brought instead to this country and contributed to so many people here.

The history of the world is pockmarked with outbreaks of antisemitism: Jews have suffered at the hands of Babylonians, Assyrians, Romans, Crusaders, Spanish Inquisition and Cossacks. But these were in bygone ages of barbarism and obscurantism, fuelled by superstitious prejudice or Christian antisemitism. In complete contrast, the Germany of the 1930s stood at the height of civilisation: art and literature abounded, universities and law-schools abounded. This was the land that produced the joy of Bach and sensitivity of Beethoven. How could it also produce Bergen-Belsen and Birkenau?

It is precisely because the terror that was unleashed was so unbelievable – and still astounds – that the rapid descent into evil must be recorded. 'The person who does not remember history is bound to live through it again,' wrote George Santayana. His words apply to many situations, but are all the more chilling when seen as a memorial plaque at Auschwitz. If the plaque that was made collectively in 1945 – 'Never again' – is to be honoured, then voices such as that of Kurt Pick must be heard.

Kurt's story is his own – but it also represents that of an entire generation whose lives were totally disrupted by the dark forces that arose in Nazi Germany and spilled over so quickly into Austria. When the storm clouds gathered in 1938, Kurt had to leave his native Vienna and seek refuge elsewhere. He left behind not only his place of birth but also the beginning of a career and set of expectations that were never to materialise. Even more devastating was the loss of his parents. But rather than just mourn the past, he started planning for the future and slowly laid down new roots.

The result was some 40 years of dedicated service in England for youngsters in need in which he touched the lives of hundreds of children. Kurt's own life had been changed irrevocably against his will, now he sought to change the lives of others for good. Throughout that time, he derived inspiration and support from the remarkable partnership that he and Pamela established – and which is still as fresh as when it started.

It means that this book serves a double purpose. First, for those who know and respect Kurt – the two tend to go together automatically – it affords a chance to learn about parts of his life with which we are not so familiar and at which we can only sit back and gasp in admiration. Second, for the general reader, it offers a unique window onto not just a remarkable personality worth knowing but an exceptional era, the reverberations of which can still be felt today in millions of lives.

Rabbi Dr Jonathan Romain

Introduction

Many true stories have been told about Jewish survivors of the Second World War. Kurt Pick's, like all of them, is both tragic and triumphant; at the same time it is also one of the more unusual. Kurt was never in a concentration camp, nor was he imprisoned in a hiding place like so many other Jews of his day. He lived – and sometimes even worked – as a fugitive in the shadows, occasionally sheltered by Belgian humanitarianism, always threatened by the terror of Hitler's persecution.

Kurt was born in Vienna in 1912, the only child of Austrian parents. His father, Alfred Pick, was the son of a Jewish glazier who lived in Patzau (Pacov in Czechoslovakian) in the centre of Bohemia, which at that time belonged to the Austrian Empire. Patzau was near Tabor, the site of a major battle fought by the Protestant Bohemians against the Roman Catholic Austrians. The Austrians had won, and in the aftermath of the fighting some of the Protestant refugees had been sheltered in the Jewish community of Patzau, into which they were assimilated and themselves became Jews.

Alfred Pick worked for a firm in Prague called Perutz which dealt in textiles, mainly cotton. In the early 1900s he was sent to Austria to establish a branch of the firm in Vienna, then the centre of the Austrian Empire. There he met his future wife, Frieda, their mothers being friends who had grown up together in Patzau's Jewish community. Frieda and her brothers and sisters were the children of a master baker who had come from Moravia and had settled eventually in the capital.

Alfred and Frieda Pick were married in 1911, and set up home together in a flat in the western outskirts of Vienna. Most residential districts were built that side of the city since the prevailing wind is from the west, while the industrial areas were sited mainly to the east. The Picks lived in a lower middle-class district largely inhabited by businessmen and civil servants. Neither of them looked or felt particularly Jewish – indeed, Frieda was very proud of her eye-catching head of red hair – rather, they had a strong sense of belonging to Viennese Austria, enabling them to fit comfortably into their surroundings.

Their acceptance in Vienna, however, did not mean that there was no anti-Jewish feeling at that time. There were, for example, no Jewish civil servants, and this prejudice extended to non-Jewish shops and schools. During the 1920s there was a family living in the flat below the Picks whose son was a friend of Kurt's. The husband was strongly antisemitic, and one day his mother-in-law came to visit them from Hartberg in Styria. She had never met a Jew, and when she saw Frieda Pick she looked her up and down, open-mouthed and eyes popping, amazed to find that she was actually looking at another human being.

Kurt began his education at the local primary school, and at ten years old went on to a grammar school, the *Real Gymnasium*. Pupils who wanted to be engineers went to a grammar which specialised in mathematics; those destined for medicine or law went to schools specialising in classics. The *Real Gymnasium* provided for both disciplines, leaving the students' options open. Only about 5 per cent of the pupils here were Jewish, and some of the teachers were openly antisemitic and pro-Nazi. There were very few Jewish teachers anyway, all of them employed in Jewish schools. At fourteen Kurt left and went to the *Alte Handels Akademie*, where the emphasis was on commerce. This school was built in the mid nineteenth century in the centre of Vienna by a prominent banker, Baron Friedrich Schey. About 70 per cent of the pupils here were Jewish and the non-Jewish teachers were tolerant.

After 1933 anti-Jewish prejudice became rife in every walk of life. *Numerus Clausus*, the scheme to limit the number of Jewish students, was being mooted openly in the right-wing press. Kurt remembers walking past the medical faculty of Vienna University one day and being surprised to see large numbers of police there. Not being permitted to enter the building uninvited, they were standing at the bottom of a flight of stairs leading up to a door into the building. A crowd of students waited in a narrow alleyway alongside. Wondering what was going on, Kurt stood and watched as well. Presently the door at the top of the stairs was flung open and two or three Jewish students were forcibly ejected and then thrown downstairs, kicked and shoved all the way down to the bottom.

On another occasion, when Kurt himself was an undergraduate, he received an urgent message from a friend who was studying in a department of the university near his own. He warned Kurt on no account to go to any lectures that day. Kurt heeded the warning and stayed at home, hearing later that another Jewish friend had been badly beaten up. Had Kurt attended his studies that day there would have been no hiding place for him: it would have been more than any of the tutors' jobs were worth to have sheltered him.

In the second half of the decade the *Anschluss* (annexation) was being pressed for by the Germans, and also by some Austrians: the incorporation of Austria into Germany. A large group of illegal members of the NSDP (Nazis) in Austria were doing their best to upset the country's economy by creating an atmosphere in which it would appear to be preferable to have Hitler running the country. They were ruthless terrorists, bombing railway lines and places which attracted large numbers of visitors in order to create panic and discourage tourism.

Kurt took his 'Matura' exams (A-levels) in every subject in 1930, and went on to university – the *Hochschule für Welthandel* – where for the next three years he studied economics, French, English, book-keeping, business management and law relating to these subjects, taking his degree, *Diplomkaufmann*, in business studies. For the first two years at university he also studied for a trade qualification in tailoring to enable him to open his own tailoring business. In fact he was one of the first people in Vienna to have both an academic and trade qualification.

Alfred Pick was insistent that his son should make his own way in the world rather than join the family business immediately, so in 1933 Kurt found himself looking for a job. He applied for one at Neumann's, a shop selling ready-made and made-to-measure tailoring for men and women in the centre of Vienna. But the economic crisis was beginning to bite and it was a time of high unemployment: the Jewish owner, Herr Neumann, interviewed him and turned him down. By chance, when Kurt arrived home to report his disappointment to his parents, a friend of the family, Frau Weninger, was visiting his mother. Her husband was the Picks' bank manager and she advised Kurt to have a word with him. Kurt duly called at the bank to be told by Herr Weninger that he was too busy to talk to him as he was just going out; Kurt, he said, had better get into the car too and tell him about it. The result was that Herr Weninger promised to contact Neumann's. Kurt applied for the job again and this time was successful. It was just one of many occasions when the Weningers proved to be two of the best friends the Picks ever had.

Despite the growing climate of menace, life for the moment continued with a fair degree of normality. Kurt went to work every day and returned home to his parents each evening with nothing worse happening to him than being grabbed off the street on one occasion and press-ganged into cleaning a flat occupied by a group of Nazis. He met with friends, listened to music and took part in sporting activities with others of his own age. Often, he would cross the road from his home and go for long walks in the *Schrebergarten*, plots of land not unlike large allotments. These were cultivated by city dwellers and often had weekend huts attached to them enabling the tenants to get out of the town for short spells.

While walking there one Sunday, Kurt was intrigued to see a crowd of men going into one of these huts empty-handed, each emerging with a parcel. He fetched his father who came at once, and together they watched unseen from a little distance. Alfred thought it looked suspicious enough for him to notify a friend who was a member of the right-wing Austrian party which was trying to prevent Austria from being annexed. He asked him to inform the Party. Kurt took the same walk again, curious to observe the outcome. Nothing happened. His father phoned the friend a second time, and was told, to his amazement, that the police had not been able to find the place; the road, they said, did not exist. Eventually, the Picks saw the police arrive, and they read in the paper next day that a large explosives depot had been found, but that most of the contents had been removed. The small amount that was left, however, had been enough to blow up half Vienna. To the Picks, this was clear evidence that the police had already been infiltrated by the Nazis.

It was just this sort of anxiety and fear for his family that took its toll of Alfred Pick's health, causing him to suffer a breakdown. Kurt left Neumann's when his father had recovered, and joined him in the family textile business. He was working there in 1938 when the Germans walked into Austria, creating such an intolerable situation for the Jews that he was forced to leave his homeland and escape into Belgium.

The war wiped out nearly all of Kurt's family, his home and his future prospects, changing radically and irrevocably the course of his life. Yet Kurt was lucky – if one can so describe someone who had the outrageous misfortune to be a Jew at that time in that place – for, as history has shown, it was against all odds that he survived. The dice seem to have been loaded in his favour from the start, for he was brought up in a home where love meant loving discipline, and of which love there was no lack. By modern standards it was perhaps a sheltered existence, but at the same time it was the best possible foundation for the hardships to come.

Three major factors have been found in helping the recovery of those who have suffered severe persecution. The first relates to the victim's age, and Kurt was at the best stage of life to withstand his experiences, having grown to manhood yet with youth and adaptability on his side, and still without the responsibility of dependants. The second is security in family life, which Kurt has in abundance in his happy marriage to Pamela. The third factor is perhaps less obvious. It concerns the great benefit derived from communicating traumatic events, however painful, to a willing listener.

This book began because Kurt was following an instinct that his story should be told. It belongs to a shameful time in the history of humanity which he believes should be remembered as an urgent warning against all racial prejudice. The evil of totalitarianism leading to genocide has not been destroyed with Hitler, and is just as dangerous by any name in any part of the world. As the work progressed, something more began to emerge which neither of us had anticipated at the beginning.

Because Kurt's parents were deported at one of the blackest moments of the war, and at a particularly stressful time for him, when what might be described as his horror threshold was at its peak, the full implication of what had happened to them did not strike him until long afterwards. As a result, for forty years he was unable to talk about his past, so that his grief remained unspoken and his mourning incomplete. It has been my privilege to listen to his story and to recount his experiences. My hope and prayer is that this book, whatever else it achieves, may serve as a channel for the healing of Kurt's memories.

In 1985 my husband and I went with Kurt and Pamela to Belgium to visit some of the people and places that feature in this book. Through the kindness of Madame Marie-Thérèse Tock-Malaise, we were able to be present at a reunion for Kurt with several other survivors whom he had not seen since the war. For me, this was not only a happy experience but a very strange one: Kurt had described these friends to me so accurately that even after nearly half a century it was like meeting people whom I too had known. It was the same with the places. We were entertained most hospitably to lunch by the Governor and his wife at the Château of Marneffe (now an open prison), where Kurt had worked as Administrator when it was a camp for Jewish refugee families. We drove through the woods to Bassines and came suddenly, as he had done, upon the archway at the entrance. It was exactly as I had pictured it. Alas, the château is no more, but peering through a little window on the right, we could see the bakery and the original brick oven where Kurt had baked bread for the school.

Strangest of all was finding the air-raid shelter at Avesnes where Kurt was nearly lynched as a German spy. We stumbled upon an aspect of it that he had never seen, but which was as clearly recognisable to me as if I had been there myself. The atmosphere of the place that Kurt's amazing memory had conjured up for me made it unmistakable.

Walking round to the front of the building, which Kurt then remembered, we were confronted by a young man who wanted to know what we were doing there. Kurt told him briefly of the tank battle that had raged overhead, and the dramatic events which he had witnessed at this now peaceful site. The lad merely shrugged his shoulders.

'What of it?' he said. 'It was a long time ago. That's all history now.'

History, indeed – Kurt's history. The rest of this book tells the story of a man with the courage to come out of the long, dark tunnel of the Holocaust with his honesty and integrity intact.

Jennifer Henderson
1998

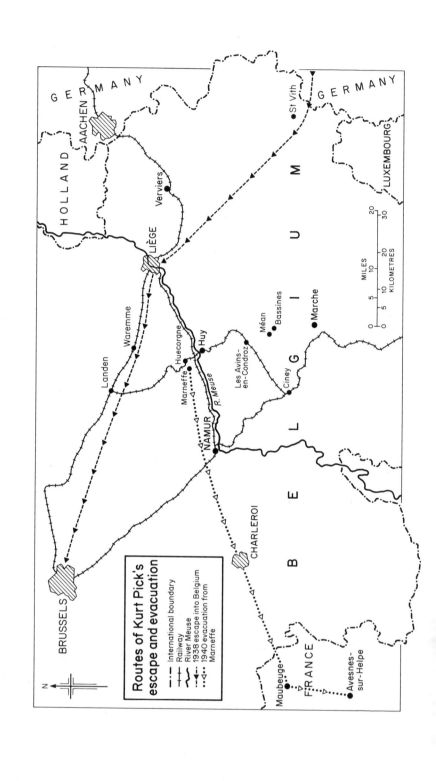

N

GERMANY

HOLLAND

AACHEN

GERMANY

St Vith

LUXEMBOURG

Verviers

LIÈGE

M

Waremme

Huecorgne

Landen

Marneffe

Huy

Méan

Bassines

Marche

R. Meuse

Les Avins-
en-Condroz

G

Ciney

NAMUR

I

U

MILES

KILOMETRES

0 5 10 20
0 5 10 20 30

L

E

BRUSSELS

CHARLEROI

B

Routes of Kurt Pick's
escape and evacuation

—··— International boundary
—+— Railway
〰️ River Meuse
▼▼ 1938 escape into Belgium
▽▽ 1940 evacuation from
      Marneffe

Maubeuge

FRANCE

Avesnes-
sur-Helpe

PART I
Brussels

CHAPTER 1

December 1938

On Christmas Eve six people were sitting in a neat, terraced house in a suburb of Aachen. To an outsider, Kurt thought, they could have been any family gathering, although in fact he had only known the dentist with his wife and little girl for a few days, while their host and hostess were strangers to them all.

The quiet, unemotional voice of the older man paused for a moment, his finger on the map spread out before him, marking a place on the border between Germany and Belgium.

'So,' he continued, as Kurt and the dentist leaned forward to see exactly where he was pointing, 'your best chance is this footpath here. It is not wide enough for vehicles and is therefore seldom used. The German Customs House is there, where you will of course get your passports exit-stamped.'

His listeners nodded their understanding. An exit stamp was essential, since it would provide the necessary evidence that they had left the country legally. Of more importance, it would prove that they had left owing nothing further in taxes or duty. On the other hand it would preclude any re-entry into Germany. Whatever happened after that, there could be no turning back. They would be forced to go ahead.

'Continue along the path and in about 20 minutes you will reach the Belgian frontier.' He looked up at their intent faces: he had come to the whole crux of the meeting. They had no visas allowing them entry into Belgium, and would have to avoid the Belgian Customs House, therefore, at all cost. His eyes returned to the map. 'As soon as you catch sight of the approach to it, turn off the path into the woods, make a wide circle under cover of the trees and rejoin the road again some-where here. Continue under this railway bridge, turn left and walk straight on until you reach the nearest station, which is in this village. Take the first train to Liège, after which you will be safe to change onto one going to Brussels.'

The speaker sat back, folding his hands, and there was silence in the little room. Presently the dentist's wife tugged gently at her husband's sleeve, pointing to the child playing quietly at their feet. They whispered together and the dentist shook his head.

Kurt endeavoured to consider dispassionately what he had just heard. There had been no question of any of them remaining in their native Austria. Since the Nazis had walked in earlier that year, Jews no longer counted as human beings, many of them already having been deported to concentration camps. In a few months the Picks had lost their home, their textile business and finally all hope for the future. Kurt had arrived in Cologne from Vienna on 23 December with the dentist and his family, all of them intending to make their way as quickly as possible into Belgium, because rumour had it that from there Jews were not yet being sent back home. They had gone to one of the hotels that still accepted Jews, to find the place so full that they had been lucky to occupy floor space in a passage. It was hardly consoling that many others were in an even worse situation, being unable to leave Germany because of unpaid taxes or lack of necessary visas. Many people had simply run out of money altogether.

Everyone was afraid to spend dwindling resources on a professional smuggler who undertook to arrange for fugitives to leave the country, in case they found themselves in the hands of a swindler. At best this would leave them penniless at a dead end; all too often it meant finishing up in a concentration camp.

Kurt weighed the pros and cons of his own dilemma. The couple in whose house he sat were retired, middle class and comfortably respectable. They looked very unlikely to be the sort of people who would betray everybody present for a quick profit. And yet the instructions had been so brief as to appear almost too simple. On the other hand the dentist, through whom the introduction had come, clearly trusted them. Apparently their credentials had satisfied him to the extent that he was prepared to gamble the safety of his wife and child on their reliability.

At this point, the dentist cleared his throat. He and his wife, he said, had decided that the risk was too great for their little daughter. She was only five and they did not think she could manage such a long walk. If they had had only themselves to consider it would have been different, but as it was, he believed they must try to find some other way.

The older man turned to Kurt. 'What about you? Will you go?'

In the end the enthusiasm of youth won the day. At twenty-six a certain degree of risk is acceptable in any adventure, and he had none of the encumbrances of the dentist. Besides, who was to know how long he might have to wait before such a promising opportunity came his way again. Meanwhile every draughty night spent on the hotel floor made further inroads into his limited pocket, which in turn left less to hazard on another chance.

'I'm game for it,' he said, 'but it would have to be today.' He had noticed that the streets were quiet; on Christmas Eve people were indoors with their families, and presumably busy with their preparations for the coming festival. By the same token he was prepared to gamble on there being fewer guards at the customs, and those on duty being just that bit slacker than usual. Surely, too, they would be more kindly disposed, less insistent upon the regulations if difficulties arose. 'Yes, *Mein Herr*, I would take you up on it and go now, this minute, while this opportunity is ripe, but it would be foolish to go alone and it seems I am the only one in favour of the plan.'

Their hostess looked at her husband with raised eyebrows and received an answering nod. She rose to her feet, saying to Kurt that if that was his only objection then it was easily solved. There was a young lady in the kitchen who was anxious to reach Antwerp. As she too had valid papers but no visa into Belgium, she was only waiting for a travelling companion such as himself.

Kurt had no time to speculate on the glamorous possibilities in store before the girl in question was brought in. She had a large, lumpy figure, round shoulders and heavy features protruding from an unspeakably bad complexion. She was perhaps the ugliest female Kurt had ever seen.

It was already early afternoon when they set out, their footsteps making little sound in the deserted streets. They walked for half an hour past lamp-lit windows, between houses that became smaller and scarcer, and at last came out into open countryside. Here the road dwindled to a stony track with ice-filled potholes and soon the forest closed in silently upon them. A little light snow began to fall, accentuating the dark recesses under the trees as if the long winter night already waited in the wings. They spoke little, the girl being gauche and nervous and both of them preoccupied with the numbing cold.

The German frontier took them by surprise as they rounded a bend to see glimpses of a hut between the trees. Kurt viewed the two guards ahead of them with mixed feelings. They were standing at ease, but they were armed and very clearly on duty. On the plus side it meant that the place was properly manned so presumably there would be no difficulty in obtaining proof of legal exit on their papers. But he saw no sign of the Christmas cheer which might have stood them in good stead later. His companion had stopped instinctively, but Kurt quickly urged her on, quietly reminding her that their papers were in order and they had nothing to worry about at this point. They walked between the two uniformed Germans, the girl's breath coming in quick, short puffs beside him, while he himself gave an exaggerated display of confidence to counterbalance the interest her nervousness might arouse.

Ten minutes later they were breathing in the resinous scent of the trees more freely, their papers duly stamped, with no awkward questions asked. They were out and on their way beyond the point of no return.

A hurried departure might still have excited suspicion, but once out of sight they lengthened their stride, Kurt taking note of the time. In a quarter of an hour the path forked and they came uncertainly to a halt. The left-hand route appeared slightly broader and more trodden, but the one on the right led more directly ahead. Kurt turned to the girl but she refused to give an opinion, gazing stubbornly at her boots. He resisted the temptation to toss a coin for fear of alarming her still further, and after a little hesitation he chose the path on the right.

In another ten minutes the light was beginning to fade and Kurt knew they should have reached the Belgian border. He cautioned the girl to slow down in case they came upon it as suddenly as they had met the German frontier. By any calculation it had taken them longer than they had been advised; also, the path seemed to be set on a perpetual right-hand bend, making it hard to tell whether they were still going in the right direction. They walked on in silence for a few more minutes and then suddenly the girl gave a little cry of dismay and clutched his arm.

She was teetering on the edge of what appeared in the half light to be an open pit alongside the path. He pulled her back, peering ahead, but their route petered out and instead, in several places, the ground gaped at their feet.

The girl shivered. 'They look like graves,' she whispered. 'What is this place?'

Kurt was about to suggest that it might be forestry when he saw something which made him turn at once and lead the way back along the path they had come. 'Quickly!' he urged her, hardly attempting to disguise his own anxiety. What they had seen had been trenches – and he had just caught sight of concrete anti-tank barriers between the trees. They had taken the wrong path and were back in Germany again. He was almost sure that they had stumbled on the Siegfried Line.

They were running now along the pale ribbon of the way ahead, Kurt grimly cursing the wasted time with its spent daylight. At the fork they stopped again. There was no certainty that this other path was the right one, and if they took another wrong turning there would be no light left. Perhaps it would be better to go back and ask the way at the German frontier, but with no right of entry now and no Belgian visas, they both shrank from doing this. Kurt did not voice his biggest fear of all: it seemed to be growing more probable every minute that their instructions had been false and that they had simply been betrayed.

Eventually, in the absence of a better idea, they set out slowly along the alternative path, aware that if it were the right one they could not be more than five minutes from the Belgian frontier. Kurt cherished no hopes of finding this one under-manned, with those on duty indoors in a convivial mood. The only difference would be that this time they approached without the necessary papers and in the darkness they would come upon it unawares.

They both jumped at the sound of footsteps close behind them, and out of the dusk they were overtaken by two workmen speaking French. These hailed them pleasantly enough, so that Kurt was encouraged to ask whether they were on the road to Belgium. To his great relief the men assured them that this was so, explaining that they were Belgians who worked in Germany going home for the night. Kurt was thinking rapidly: it was more than likely that, innocently or otherwise, these men would mention seeing them to the customs guards. It was necessary, therefore, to take them into his confidence and beg them to say nothing about meeting two strangers. The men agreed without demur and offered to do more; they would walk on ahead, they said, and light a cigarette as a sign that they had reached the guards.

Kurt and the girl followed at a safe distance and presently the tiny flame of a lighter flared up and was extinguished. They stepped quickly off the path and felt their way in among the trees, aware of a conversation going on at the Customs House which they were too far away to understand. The voices ceased, and suddenly two much larger shafts of light appeared and began to move steadily towards them.

At first Kurt was unwilling to believe that they had been betrayed, but the torches were sweeping the undergrowth and the sound of heavy boots trampling the brushwood was coming nearer and nearer. He pushed the girl into a patch of evergreens and whispered to her to keep still, but it was not big enough to hide both of them. He himself half crawled, half ran further into the forest, hunting desperately for anything leafy enough to cover him. At last he came to a thicket of overgrown saplings and plunged in, crouching among them. In spite of the cold the sweat of fear and exertion poured off his back and chest, and presently in the freezing air his teeth began to chatter.

There was a sudden shout, then a piercing squeal and the torches converged on a dark mass of spruce. The girl, crying pitifully, was dragged out – caught like a rabbit in the headlamps of a car. Kurt was aching all over now, and his knees were in such an agony of cramp he could not have moved had there been time to run away. He watched the torches sweeping ever closer, the bareness of winter leading them swiftly from cover to cover until it seemed certain that they must surely hear his panting breath between his clattering jaws. One of the guards was so close now that Kurt could have reached out and touched his arm as he bent back the branches to search the pools of darkness underneath.

The moisture had seeped into Kurt's socks where, unprotected by his outer clothing, they now froze stiffly to his ankles. He no longer exercised any control over his numbed feet, and, shrinking a little further into the bushes, he lost his balance and snapped a twig as he moved.

Instantly, the guard turned. The torch shone full in Kurt's face and strong hands closed upon his arms.

Rather to Kurt's surprise, the customs officers were not brutes and took no delight in having made a capture. On the contrary, they were pleasant, ordinary men, even reasonably sympathetic to the prisoners. At first it seemed as if they might be persuaded to open the door and look the other way; they agreed that it was an impossible position to be stuck between two countries with no inward papers for either, and that it had been rough luck being caught so near success. But they were sorry, no documents meant no entry; they had a job to do and that was all there was to it.

Kurt wheedled in vain, reminding them that it was Christmas the next day, and that surely this was the season of good will. He looked from one to the other and saw only slight surprise and a hardening of attitude as they shook their heads with a shrug. It began to dawn on Kurt that he had made a mistake. Christmas with its spirit of festivity had been left behind in his homeland; here, he was a whole week too early to cash in on the celebration of the New Year. He changed tactics: did the guards realise what they were condemning them to if they sent them back? Yes, it seemed they did know, and they were sorry to have to do it – they had already said so.

Kurt began to plead with them, begging for mercy. They would, he pointed out, have this on their consciences for ever after. The girl was crying now, while the younger of the guards, a big handsome fellow, watched her indifferently. Kurt wished helplessly that his companion had been blessed with the kind of looks that excited a man's interest. A pretty face might yet have charmed the way to freedom for them both; as it was, the guards' expressions showed only growing distaste for the redness of her nose and blotchy skin. Kurt's fruitless pleading began to sound monotonous; their captors were getting impatient. Quite clearly they despised the prisoners, who had nothing to commend them and were becoming a nuisance. He and the girl were simply not worth preserving.

When the guard changed for the night the two captives were escorted down to the village and delivered to the frontier station on the main road back to Aachen. After a brief conversation between the officials they were led out again into the biting cold and halted at the east-bound tram stop. When the tram arrived they were pushed inside while the driver was instructed on no account to let them out before they had reached Germany.

The door was shut fast on Kurt's hoarse pleading with the guards, and even the girl's sobbing ceased, her hands covering her face in total capitulation. There was a sudden silence. Everyone on board was staring at the newcomers, including the driver, who evidently saw no good reason for transporting people free merely because they were unwilling to travel.

'Aachen Station?' he suggested.

Obediently, they bought two tickets and the tram moved on. Full circle, thought Kurt. A day trip to Belgium and back at the cost of his legal departure from Germany and his freedom. Gone, too, were his optimism, his sense of adventure and his youthful zest. The sortie had been a complete failure; he was done for and there was no more fight left in him.

A few minutes later the tram stopped again at the German border. Here, too, was another customs office, and if Kurt's spirits could have plummeted any lower they would have done so, for this one was manned by brown-shirted Nazi SA men. The tram door slammed back and there was a raucous shout from the pavement: 'Juden raus!' ('Jews out!')

Slowly, Kurt and the girl left their seats and made their way to the door, fumbling for what documents they had. Kurt held his passport tightly in his hand, anxious to demonstrate that all was in order, but as they crossed the threshold he nearly let it slip through his fingers at the shock of what he saw. The room was filled with people, all of them Jews, all frightened and all caught in the same net. He began, haltingly, to explain that they had been travelling in good faith, that they had valid passports and had not intended to come back into Germany...

But the SA man who had called them was not listening, nor was he studying the documents held out for his inspection. He was looking past them, out of the door to the tram still waiting patiently for its two absent passengers. His eyes returned to Kurt. Had they, he enquired, paid to go as far as the station? Kurt replied that they had. The Nazi brightened. That was good; in that case they could go by tram to the station and leave more room in the van for all these others. They were to report to the SA at the station and wait for the rest of the prisoners there. And then he simply pushed them out again.

Kurt and the girl got back onto the tram. They did not speak, but when they came to a place Kurt recognised just before the station they got out, and no one barred their way. As the tram disappeared round a corner the girl said quietly that she knew of a small hotel near there which took Jews, and suggested that they went to it.

The place was full to bursting. As Kurt lay dozing and listening and dozing again he was not sure whether the endless procession of feet which stepped over him, round him and onto him was really a part of the people and voices that kept waking him, or only a part of his uneasy dreams. At the front of his mind was the knowledge that his name and description had been registered at several different offices that day. He was a marked fugitive, and the places where he could hide were few and must be well known to the Gestapo. A dozen times that night he heard a banging at the street door, and lay holding his breath with the sweat breaking out of him in the darkness, in case the brown-shirts had hunted him and traced him and come for him.

On Christmas morning Kurt walked alone to the station. His face was muffled in a scarf, the biting wind reason enough for his bent shoulders and bowed head. There were few people in the streets, and the ticket office and the railway platforms also were practically deserted, making him feel all

the more conspicuous. He was painfully conscious that anyone who saw him might recognise him, and found himself –
quite unreasonably – expecting to see the brown-shirts of the
night before still waiting at the station to arrest him. He
bought a ticket to Cologne from behind his handkerchief in
the husky accents of a sore throat, and retired to the lavatory
until the train was due.

Back in Cologne his morale improved immeasurably to
find the dentist and his family still at the same hotel. They
greeted him with relief too, owning that they felt no little
responsibility to his parents for his safety, and together they
found a quiet corner in which to discuss the next move. In
theory they were back to square one; in practice the situation
was now even more difficult. After a false start with a dead-
end money was tighter, suspicion towards other professional
smugglers greater. They had to find another way out, with
one less avenue open to them. On the credit side, they were
reunited, and they all had family backing in Vienna, which
meant financial help if it were needed. In spite of this Kurt
knew that any optimism would be quite unfounded.

During Kurt's absence the dentist had met someone else
from Vienna whose friend had managed to get to Brussels
from Cologne. That afternoon he introduced this young man
to his wife and Kurt, explaining that he had tracked down the
people who had arranged the smuggling. These could produce a car in two or three days time which would be able to
take the passengers to the Belgian frontier, whence they
would be escorted across the border to a railway station.
With the owner of the car and a co-driver they would number
seven, a tight fit even though one was only a child; also, the
price was high. Nevertheless, the offer was accepted almost
immediately, and a few days later the fugitives received a message to wait on the street corner of a certain square for the car
which would come and stop beside them at half past twelve
in the middle of the day.

Buoyed up by the prospect of further activity, Kurt had
been the first to declare himself in favour of the plan. It had
already been proved sound by the young man who had

reached Brussels, it would be carried out in the company of trusted friends and was deemed practical even for a five-year-old. Now, standing in the penetrating wind as they waited for the car, his enthusiasm began to ebb. How could one be sure of any scheme working with all the rumours that were flying about? No one had discovered where on the frontier they would be taken, or how they would proceed from there. He and the dentist had concluded instantly that the railway station would be Liège, but there was nothing to confirm this. It occurred to him now that it might be some far less convenient place, perhaps, where they would be fatally conspicuous. He knew nothing about this stranger who had arranged it all – and even less about the driver of the car.

Kurt turned up his coat collar and shivered as he looked up and down the road, seeing no sign of the car which was already ten minutes late. If they had been cheated they were all extremely vulnerable, exposed not only to the wintry weather but also to public view from all directions. They had just what they stood up in, and when the smugglers had taken their dues their pockets would be virtually empty. Any surplus money had had to be sent home to comply with the strict laws governing the export allowance. It was 12.45 and not a car to be seen.

By ten-to-one a few snowflakes had begun to drive into their faces and the little girl was whimpering and pulling on her parents' hands. The young man looked grey and pinched with anxiety as he murmured over and over again, 'I cannot understand it; I made so sure it was foolproof.'

Presently Kurt heard a distant clock strike and gave up any further hope. They must face the fact that no car was coming, and start all over again. He turned to the dentist to suggest that they should split up and return to the hotel along separate routes in case they had been observed. At that moment a car drew up to the kerb alongside them, the man in the passenger seat reached behind him and opened the door, and without a word the five of them squeezed into the back.

The euphoria lasted for about a couple of hours. There was very little traffic and they were soon clear of the town and its suburbs and were travelling through villages interspersed with open countryside. Nobody spoke; the passengers were so tightly packed they had hardly room to breathe. Kurt, sandwiched between the other young man and the dentist's wife with the child on her knee, could see very little of the two men in front. There was no doubt, however, that they were familiar with the route, and their confidence was infectious: the passengers relaxed, thankful to be on their way at last.

Kurt opened his eyes when the child grew restless and whispered something to her mother.

'Oh no, darling,' the dentist's wife replied, 'I'm afraid we cannot stop here. We still have a long way to go.' The answer revealed the request, and Kurt sympathised silently with the predicament of each. The dentist took his little girl onto his lap and wiped the mist off the window, showing her that it was snowing, to divert her attention.

It was coming down hard out of a leaden sky, sticking to the windscreen so that the wipers groaned and jerked to clear it. The driver glanced, frowning, at his colleague, and muttered something, and Kurt sensed their sudden apprehension as the other leant forward to assess this unscheduled hazard. They were climbing now in the ever-increasing whiteness; Kurt could hear the whine of the tyres on each bend, while the cold, seeping in despite each others' close proximity, added to the general discomfort.

The daylight was fading early and the road grew steeper. The driver negotiated several hairpin bends at a speed which set the passengers wincing, and then accelerated slightly to tackle a long, straight hill on which the snow lay several inches deep. The engine revved, the back wheels spinning sideways into the middle of the road. The car, steered into the skid, lost speed and came to a standstill, the wheels still spinning fruitlessly in the freshly-fallen snow.

The two men in front got out and walked round to see what could be done, while Kurt and the other young man opened a door at the back to offer help. At that moment a party of about eight young people coming from the opposite direction drew up alongside, and the passengers were quickly pushed back inside with instructions to everyone to keep quiet and not to show their faces. The youngsters came across and asked what was the trouble, whereupon the two drivers eagerly took them up on their offer of a push. Presently, with much revving of the engine and shoving from behind, the car moved on, gathering speed and holding the road once more.

'Arbeitsdienst,' said the dentist. The help had come from members of the Labour Service, young people drafted into work by the Nazis. Kurt read the same thought in each of the faces round him: what would their rescuers' reaction have been had they known that they had just helped a car load of Jews flee the country?

The dentist's little girl could not be sidetracked any longer. At first she fidgeted, then she became fretful and finally she broke into continuous crying. She was tired, frustrated and miserably uncomfortable, as indeed were they all. They bumped and slid and shivered, sick with fatigue, their joints enduring positions no longer tenable, because they could do nothing about it. At six o'clock the driver announced that they should have arrived at the border by now, but that owing to the state of the weather they still had about another hour and a half to go. Kurt could happily have leaned forward and strangled him at the wheel.

Shortly before 7.30 the car stopped on a quiet, unlit stretch of road. The drivers presented their account, the bill was paid, and after another ten minutes' driving they arrived at the German frontier post. Kurt slipped his passport among the others, hoping that the exit stamp on his alone might pass unnoticed, and found to his relief that the officials here were more interested in the amount of money and goods leaving the country. All of them were frisked and everyone received an exit stamp without demur.

They stepped out into the night to find themselves on the bank of a river which formed the border there. Ahead of them a wide, well-lit bridge carried the road across to the forbidden territory of Belgium. The two drivers led the way along a footpath at the edge of the water until they came to a railway bridge, where they stopped. Then, having instructed their followers to wait, they left them and were swallowed up immediately in the darkness.

Kurt and his little party waited. It had stopped snowing but the frost gripped their hands and feet. The moonlight, filtering through a few breaks in the cloud, scribbled jagged patterns on the black surface of the water. Beyond that they could see nothing in the freezing silence.

They waited. Kurt tried to recall the faces of the two drivers, and could not. They had been nondescript, quite unmemorable; just two highly efficient professionals doing a job. And for this they had been paid a considerable sum of money with which they had vanished without trace, leaving the customers still on the wrong side of the frontier. With mounting suspicion Kurt recollected their undoubted knowledge of the route and their accurate timing of the journey. Added to this, the customs officers had seemed to know them almost as if their visit were a routine occurrence. He wondered bleakly how many others had stood where they now stood, and for how long before they too had realised that they had been tricked.

Suddenly one of the drivers reappeared out of the darkness beside them. With him was another man, a Belgian, who led the way onto the railway bridge, ordering them to follow. There was no footpath and the sleepers were covered with a treacherous coating of rime; between each was a gap wide enough to trap a man's foot, with a sheer drop into the river below. The dentist hurriedly picked up his little daughter, now barely conscious with exhaustion, and together they shuffled their way across the bridge, clinging to the icy handrail, their knees trembling with the cold and the effort required.

On the opposite bank they were greeted by two more Belgians – and a dog who sniffed the air intently, ears pricked. Kurt could see lights in a nearby house, and at a little distance a ribbon of light along a road over another bridge. He could see nothing else and there was not a sound to be heard.

Presently, on a word of command the dog bounded away, returning after a brief absence to sit at his master's feet.

The Belgian said softly that it was trained to sniff out police and officials and give a warning. It was safe, now, to go to the house.

The relief was indescribable, and of every kind. They had arrived in Belgium – only just, but nevertheless, they had crossed the border – and here at last was the long-denied pause for their more intimate needs, before the wife of one of the men brought them hot soup and a loaf of bread where they sat in the warmth of the stove. When the Belgians raised the subject of the continuation of their journey, Kurt had to wrench his concentration back to the business in hand. One of them was describing a footpath over the hills which would involve several hours' strenuous walking, and he admitted it would be even more arduous after the snow-falls during the day.

The dentist looked at his little family and shook his head in despair, while his wife begged the other woman to find some easier way to help them. They were already so tired, she said, and would have to carry the little one.

The woman hesitated and then suggested to her husband that they could take them by car to a railway station. At Liège, for instance, it was unlikely that they would be asked for any papers.

The Belgian came straight to the point. 'How much money do you have?'

The dentist emptied his pockets onto the table and the other young man followed suit. Kurt, seeing nothing else for it, pulled out enough to match the others, managing to leave behind his gold signet ring. The two Belgians turned to the dentist's wife with an interest that was entirely professional. They accepted without argument that she had no more cash, but they suggested that she might have something else to contribute. Slowly, she removed her ring and added it to the rest. The warmth of hospitality had cooled suddenly to the temperature of the world outside.

One of the Belgians said gravely that that was just about enough.

He was speaking, had he known it, to an exceedingly wealthy woman. Not for nothing was she married to a dentist: every molar she possessed had been filled with a diamond.

Soon after midnight they set out for Liège. Kurt was surprised to find a car waiting at the door, as if it had been a foregone conclusion that they would continue their journey by road. They clambered in on top of one another as before, and the car moved off very slowly, without lights, towards the road that had been visible on their arrival. There was just enough moonlight reflected from the snow for the driver to make out the lane ahead of him, and in a few minutes they came to a T-junction with the bridge over the river to the left. The Belgian turned right, switching on the headlamps and changing up swiftly into top gear. In spite of the load it carried, the car responded immediately, saying much for the power beneath the bonnet. The cold night air began to find its way through to the passengers, cutting across the stupor of weariness, and soon Kurt was wide awake again, aware that they were travelling at speed along a straight, well-lit road.

Suddenly, two *gendarmes* appeared in the middle of the road ahead, flagging them down. This is it, thought Kurt: the moment of reckoning has come at last. Then the driver jumped viciously on the accelerator and steered straight at the men. For a second they held their ground, waving for all they were worth, but as the car kept its course, gathering speed and bearing down upon them, at the last minute they leapt for safety.

Kurt observed the incident with the detachment of suspended belief. Light-headed with strain and fatigue, he felt all the exhilaration of adventure with none of the anxiety of participation. He was elated at the thought of the tale he would have to tell, but it was no more real to him than if he had been watching a gangster film: the Belgian smugglers had outwitted the authorities, and Kurt, himself the precious contraband, sped on unhindered through the night.

Two hours later they entered Liège, and at about three o'clock the car arrived at the station. The drivers remained seated, quietly discussing something in a patois none of those in the back understood. Presently one of them got out, instructing his colleague not to allow anyone to leave the car. Much later Kurt realised the reason for this errand: it was necessary to find out whether a certain road rising steeply out of Liège was passable in the present weather conditions. At the time he consoled himself with the knowledge that the Belgians were no keener to be caught in their company than were those they smuggled.

The other reappeared shortly, and with an abrupt 'We are taking you to Brussels,' they were once more on the move. At about 6.30, in the grey beginnings of daylight, they were put out onto the pavement, shivering and aching, to walk to the young man's friend in whose steps they had just followed.

Here Kurt spent his first hour in Brussels. It was a dark little house and the friend's room at the top of it smelt damp and musty. Plaster flaked from the walls onto the rough floor boards and the torn scrap of cloth which served for a curtain trembled in the draught round the ill-fitting window frame. They arranged themselves, one on the solitary chair and the rest along the edge of the iron bedstead, while their bony, haggard host produced coffee to be shared from two cracked cups.

The romance of his escape, like the journey itself, was over. Kurt sat stupefied as the young man's friend began to issue advice that the newcomers would do well to take. He made an effort to listen but as each phrase penetrated his exhausted mind it was involuntarily rejected. The gist of what he heard was as bleak as the room in which he sat – a stark reminder that the future for which he had staked everything would be ultimately nothing but squalour and degradation.

Yet he had won. Against all odds, he had made this journey; he had crossed the border and he had arrived at his chosen destination. He had established himself as a survivor.

Relief welled up in him.

CHAPTER 2

December 1938-June 1939

There is a time beyond tiredness and hunger when the body seems to have forgotten how to hanker for sleep and food. Kurt, sitting in the small boarding house near the Gare du Nord, where he had walked with the dentist and his family, found himself hardly interested in the bread that had been put before him. There was coffee, too, and that he swallowed in great scalding gulps, and felt warmed and revived.

The dentist's friends, Herr and Frau Sonntag, sat with them while they breakfasted, reiterating the advice Kurt remembered only vaguely hearing earlier that morning. Now, with the second wind provided by the hot drink, he was able to put the shock of his arrival in Brussels behind him and listen to all that was being said. Thus, an hour later he was out on the street again, making his way towards the offices of the Jewish Refugee Committee, where he needed to enrol for regular subsistence. Here he would be helped to find somewhere to live, and be issued with a little money week by week, enabling him, if he were arrested, to prove that he had some financial support at a time of high unemployment.

This in itself would not be a safeguard against deportation, for Belgium was under no obligation to admit illegal immigrants, as Kurt knew only too well from recent experience. But the government of the time was inclined to a humanitarian attitude, and anyone picked up without a valid identity card stood a good chance of being issued with an official document giving him three months in which to leave the country. These *feuilles de route* could often be renewed, provided nothing was known against the holder; nevertheless, he was warned, there were those who, for no apparent reason, had failed to obtain an extension and had been deported. Ultimately, nothing was certain: Kurt would be lucky if he acquired the security of three months' notice to quit, and luck carries with it no guarantee.

The offices of the Jewish Committee were in a shabby building down a side road in a poor area of Brussels. This was unofficially the Jewish Quarter, but there was nothing to make Kurt feel he belonged here. While the girl at the desk gave him the necessary money together with the addresses of a few cheap rooms to let, he became aware that the chatter had almost ceased around him. Furtive glances were cast in his direction, both inside the building and from those in little groups who stood about outside, and presently he found himself at the centre of half a dozen eager faces, all pressing closer to him, all asking questions and offering further advice of every kind. His was fresh blood, ripe for sharing, and the realisation of this only enhanced his feeling of strangeness among them. The place clearly formed quite a club, but it was not one that held any attraction for Kurt who thought of himself as primarily an Austrian refugee. These people were almost all Eastern Jews, isolated and inward looking, Jewish by birth but Zionist by dream. Kurt pocketed his weekly money along with the razor and soap which formed his only luggage, and having enquired at the desk where he could find the main post office, he left as quickly as possible.

The business now uppermost in his mind was to telephone his parents and reassure them of his safe arrival. The job of finding a room could wait; it was still only mid-morning and there would be plenty of time later in the day to visit the handful of addresses he had been given. He walked into the centre of the city along wide boulevards and well-kept squares, and found the Central Telephone Office on a corner of the place de Brouckère. Here he asked for a connection to Vienna and learned that all the lines were jammed and there would be a long delay.

He settled down to study the list of accommodation provided while he waited. The rooms available were cheap and in poor districts; moreover all of them, necessarily, were owned by people who were prepared to flout the laws of registration and conceal the presence of a tenant from the police. It was imperative for him to find a house owned by someone who would do this because he himself was Jewish, the motive for secrecy being often much less straightforward. Many of those with rooms to let were involved in activities of a kind that prompted the police to make frequent calls checking on visiting strangers, and Kurt was terrified that if he took a room in such a house he would count as an accessory in the event of a raid. He ran the risk of falling foul of the law simply by mixing with criminals, and as an offender he could not hope to be granted permission to remain in Belgium. This, he had been warned, was just the sort of situation to cause his luck to run out.

He waited five hours before his call came through. Then, for a few brief rejoicing moments, he forgot everything else as he shared with his parents their intense relief.

He woke from a dream of Vienna to the cold reality of Brussels.

By the time Kurt left the Central Telephone Office it was quite dark and too late to go hunting for somewhere to live. He decided to return to the Sonntags for the night and to look for a room next morning. It did not bother him that he had not memorised the address; he knew it was near the Gare du Nord and was sure he could find it from there.

But the city had taken on an entirely different aspect by night and after so many hours indoors he recognised nothing. Remembering the big boulevard by which he had approached the Central Telephone Office, he was not surprised to see brightly lit shops across the street. What he had forgotten was that the entrance was not in the Central Boulevard but round the corner in a side road. Had it been daylight he might have noticed that these shops were smaller and less pretentious than those in the main street, but lit up to attract the passing world they seemed to dazzle with no less magnificence. Consequently, thinking he was in the Central Boulevard, he turned right and began to walk east instead of north. He passed the end of the main shopping centre in the rue Neuve and went briskly on, quite satisfied that he was heading in the right direction.

Suddenly the civilised world of shops and electricity came to an abrupt end and he was plunged into darkness. Puzzled, Kurt walked on a little; perhaps this was just an alley which would open out into a wider road. Presently he stumbled. There was not a glimmer of light ahead, so he turned down a slightly bigger road to the left and then, convinced he was now heading too far west, he turned right. After a few minutes he had to admit to himself that he was hopelessly lost. He considered returning to the post office and starting again, only to realise he had no idea by what route he had come.

He walked on, peering about him in the darkness in the hope of seeing a familiar landmark, and after what seemed hours of drifting he came to a wide, well-lit road that he was quite certain he had never seen before. It was, in fact, the circular boulevard that runs right round Brussels, but to his confused senses it came as the final defeat. He was totally lost in a strange city. It was bitterly cold, he had very little money and nowhere to spend the night. He had no notion of the address of the only people he knew, and since he spoke very little French he was obliged to treat everyone as potentially likely to call for his arrest.

Such was his disorientation that he felt confident only that the general direction he wanted was to the right. Accordingly, he set off once more, but as he still recognised nothing, it seemed that the only course open to him was to ask someone. He looked around with great reluctance, knowing that his limited French betrayed him immediately as a foreigner, and chose a young couple strolling arm-in-arm. Surely, he thought, they could not possibly have the remotest connection with the police. He accosted them politely and in halting, school-boy French asked the way to the Gare du Nord.

To his amazement they pointed back the way that he had come. This was too much: his head reeled as he tried to turn over his whole notion of Brussels. Wondering whether perhaps they had not understood him, he thanked them and waited until they were out of sight before picking on another harm-less looking character and requesting a second opinion. Without hesitation this man too waved an arm in the same direction. Completely mystified, and not entirely convinced even then, Kurt obediently turned and retraced his steps.

He found the station, and with it his bearings. From there it was a short walk to the road he wanted, the name of which he then remembered. He recognised the boarding house instantly: it was in a plain little terrace in a dull part of town, but at that moment no palace had ever looked more beautiful.

The girl who came to the door was puzzled when Kurt asked for the Sonntags. He repeated the name and then she nodded. Ah yes, she remembered them now – but she was sorry, they were no longer staying there. They had left that afternoon.

He woke before daylight because the floor was hard and he was very cold. For a while he lay there not knowing what room it was nor how he came to be in it; then he remembered the maid finding the Sonntags' new address for him. It had been nine o'clock by the time he had settled down for the night on the floor-space offered him.

An early tram rumbling past the end of the road stirred recollections of his childhood. The sound took him straight back to the first-floor flat in the house where he had been brought up. He closed his eyes again in an effort to recapture the memories and to savour for a little longer the essential quality of home they had evoked. Already the image was fading, but in his mind he still stood at the open living-room window, looking out at the crimson buds of the lime trees all along the road, just opening in a flourish of young green leaves, while the scent of a deep purple lilac drifted up to him, filling the room with its fragrance. The warmth of the spring sunshine touched the familiar things of his childhood: the solid mahogany centre table, the fine white hand-embroidered linen curtains, and the sofa where his father invariably spent 15 minutes after lunch, a long thin cigar in his mouth and a gallery of pictures on the wall above him.

Kurt remembered with peculiar clarity the arrival of the latest of these pictures a few years earlier. It had been his mother's birthday and they had all gathered a little early for lunch. Alfred Pick brought a large, flat parcel from the bedroom and hid it furtively behind a chair while Frieda was putting the finishing touches to the meal. Every time she passed by on her way to receive more flowers and messages from friends and neighbours at the door, she averted her eyes from the parcel; only when all her preparations were complete did Alfred produce his present.

Kurt was highly amused at her squeals of surprise. There was little enough room to hide anything in the flat; she could hardly have failed to know about something of that size – indeed he suspected she had already peeped inside more than once – but her pleasure as she pulled off the wrapping paper was undoubtedly genuine.

The parcel contained a painting by Larwin, a contemporary Austrian genre artist much admired by Frieda. It depicted a street scene with a washerwoman carrying a basket, her apron tucked up over a colourful Austrian *dirndl* skirt. She was young and blonde; against the background of houses two *pulcher* (rough-necks), watched her with a lively interest. The freshness of her youth and natural beauty appealed instantly to Frieda, just as Alfred had anticipated. Proudly he confided details of how he had learned of it, tracked it down, bargained with the dealer, bought it and finally hidden it – she would never, never guess where! And Frieda, to her eternal credit, opened her eyes wide and did not guess, although Kurt glimpsed a flash of something that was not exactly innocence as she turned her red head quickly back to the picture.

So the painting had been hung with pride on an already overcrowded wall, and his parents had gone off once more to the office on the tramway that looped round the house and returned to the city.

Kurt sat up, wide awake, coughing in the dust of the floor.

The first room on the list he had been given of possible lodgings was in the rue Brogniez near the Gare du Midi, not far from the offices of the Jewish Refugee Committee. It was in one of those narrow, terraced houses that are three rooms deep, the middle one having no window, like the inside cabin on board ship. Kurt was shown the second floor back attic, where the only daylight came through a small skylight. There was no ceiling and freezing draughts penetrated the gaps in the roof beyond the rafters. The furniture consisted of an ancient iron bedstead with two cheap blankets and a grubby little pillow, a rickety table and chair and a battered chest of drawers that had once been painted white, on which stood a chipped enamel bowl and jug. As Kurt looked round in some dismay, the landlady switched on a naked light bulb briefly, as if to emphasise that electricity was being thrown in. On the way downstairs she indicated an insalubrious apology for plumbing. The package was on offer for about a quarter of his monthly allowance.

Kurt took the room without looking further afield. He had no reason to suppose that the others would be any better, and he felt satisfied that here at least the owners were honest and he would be in no danger of blackmail. They were an Eastern Jewish couple with a son and a daughter, comfortably off with a wholesale business fixing metal frames to handbags in workshops on the premises. Communication threatened to be a problem as, to their surprise, Kurt did not speak Yiddish, but with the aid of a little miming they all got by with bits of three languages. Indeed, he soon discovered that his landlady found it more difficult to stay silent: she was anxious to impress her lodger with every opportunity to show him that she was mistress of the art of gracious living.

At the frozen summit of the house, Kurt would have welcomed life being a little more gracious to himself. Since the attic was unheated and there was no insulation in the roof, he might as well have been camping in a barn. Having nothing else to wear, he had to sleep in his clothes, using his gabardine overcoat with its woollen lining as an extra blanket. It was the only warm garment he had and, coming from a well-heated flat in Vienna, he shivered morning, noon and night. For a day or two he contemplated washing one item of clothing at a time and suspending it from a rafter to drip, but the prospect of the icy water and the impossibility of drying anything thoroughly, let alone doing without it meanwhile, was too daunting. So he wore the same clothes 24 hours a day, seven days a week, and thought grimly that if he did not stink it was only because there was no chance of sweating at that temperature.

His landlady at any rate apparently noticed nothing untoward about him, and seemed rather to be intrigued by him than to despise him. Evidently she wondered what such a well-bred young man was doing in an attic like that. Kurt guessed that she and her husband were immigrants, an ordinary family from a small Jewish community in Eastern Europe. Her airs and graces betrayed her awareness of the difference in culture between them, a difference she did not understand but was ever at pains to conceal. Clearly, in her own eyes she had bettered herself beyond belief, living in a brick house with running water and a staircase, on an income which permitted weekly outings with friends in the cheap new finery of her dreams. She was an enthusiastic movie-goer at a time when cinemas were palaces of luxury and opulence, and Kurt's envy of these visits knew no bounds. He longed to sit and watch the programme round as many times as it was shown, just to experience the warmth and comfort provided. But most of the time he could have scraped up barely enough for the customary tip to the usherette, and had to make do with a few precious minutes by the kitchen stove while he admired the chic of his landlady pirouetting in front of him before she set out.

Soon she spotted that he had the additional charm of education, and this led to a whole new area of acquaintance. Her thirteen-year-old daughter was at a grammar school, and she suggested that Kurt might be interested to see a sample of the work expected of the child. He was to understand, of course, that it was in no way a reflection on the girl that she could not do her homework, but rather that at such a superior school the standard was so exceptionally high – especially, it seemed, in mathematics. Kurt nodded wisely and joined the hapless teenager in the warmth of the kitchen with alacrity. Once inside, he found no difficulty in assuring her mother that the problems were indeed extremely hard and she was not to be surprised if the explanation took a long time. His efforts were rewarded by a mug of hot coffee, wonderfully welcome in spite of the skin, at which he would have shuddered back in Vienna. With it came the ultimate in luxury: sugar, in as great a quantity as Kurt could ladle into it while both their backs were turned.

Upstairs, life on his own was not so sweet. He had to budget meticulously, setting aside the rent and spending almost the whole of the rest of his allowance on food. Once in a while he would treat himself to the cheapest available hot meal on the first floor of Sarma's Stores, but for the most part the least expensive restaurant was way beyond his means. The only way to get enough to eat was to buy food, and as bread and milk offered the best value in nourishment, he rationed himself to a monotonous diet of half a loaf and a litre of milk per day. Even so, the Belgian bread was of a lighter texture than that baked in Vienna, more refined and weight-for-weight less satisfying. He became obsessed by food, unable to think of anything else as he counted the minutes until he might allow himself a few more mouthfuls of each dwindling portion. More than once he felt grateful for his old-fashioned upbringing that enabled him to impose the strict self-discipline needed to keep something back for the following day. If he managed to save any money he spent it on broken biscuits, dividing the sweet fragments into as many separate treats as he could bear to stretch them.

Hunger, like the cold, bit deeply into him. There were many stories going round of people in the same situation disintegrating under the strain. He determined not to yield to the temptation of remaining in bed until it was virtually impossible to get up and take action against the inevitable alternative of slow starvation. Even so, there was common sense in not starting the day too early. A few extra hours under the covers meant retaining any body heat generated overnight for a little longer; it meant fewer hours out in the cold and so fewer precious calories expended. The greatest advantage, though, was that breakfast could be cut almost without being missed. By staying in bed until mid-morning he not only saved on valuable energy, but needed to cater for a whole meal less each day.

All the same, it still left many hours to be filled while his stomach was not, and there was little to take his mind off the deficit. When he walked along the road he found himself drawn against his will to the windows of shops that sold food, especially bakeries. There he would stand for as long as he could bear it, gazing in at the sweet pastries, the rich cakes covered thickly with powdered sugar, the glazed apricot and apple tarts side by side with eclairs and meringues bulging with *crème pâtissière*. He developed the art of positioning himself so that whenever the door was opened the comforting aroma of baking flowed out to submerge him in a homely nostalgia of delicacies beyond the wildest limits of his pocket. But it was unwise to attract attention by standing still anywhere for very long, and soon he would have to wander on in the sobering chill of the winter air, hour after hour till his hands and his feet ached with the cold, pinning all his remaining hope on the possibility of the grammar school setting maths for homework again that evening.

Gradually, like stars on a frosty night, tiny pinpricks of comfort began to appear in his life. He started to receive letters from home, and once, in answer to a request for something with which to heat water, his mother sent him an electric beaker which plugged into the light socket and heated one cup of liquid. He splashed out on a small jar of Horlicks and when life was more than usually bleak he would treat himself to a hot, malted drink that did much to restore his morale.

But hunger and cold were not the only, or even the worst, enemies as he lay curled up on his bed for the length of the bitter, unlit evenings. He was twenty-seven, intelligent and cultured, a personable young man who had been well liked among a wide circle of friends in Vienna. Now, whole days would pass without hearing the sound of his own voice, without seeing a face he recognised. At a time of life when it is normal to be surrounded by friends, Kurt found himself totally isolated. The relentless need for hot, satisfying food and thicker clothes nagged him less than a craving for human contact, and he missed no creature comfort more acutely than companionship, and particularly the company of a pretty girl.

Little by little he came to realise that he was not alone in his loneliness. He began to see the same people here and there, collecting weekly dues at the Jewish Refugee Committee, sauntering along the frozen streets, loitering with the same lack of intent as himself, interminably padding out the empty days of nothingness. Theirs too, he discovered, was a fantasy world of unfulfilled dreams, a world of which he had become a part. Like them he saw a mirage of escape – in his case to Australia – once he had acquired the necessary visa and money. Like them he still believed in such a goal, even though the likelihood of attaining it slipped ever further from him as the days went by. There were those who had waited infinitely longer than he had, others who no longer had the strength even to dream, and he himself fought a desperate battle against hopelessness, inertia and disintegration. Meanwhile, he learnt to listen, to snatch at rumours, to sift and to discern between them, for in this way information was disseminated, contacts were made – and a whisper plucked out of the air could be used to take another step towards his goal.

He discovered that many refugees clubbed together regularly for a midday meal cooked by hosts for a modest sum. One of these groups Kurt joined, and although the meals were pitifully simple they were not only hot but they provided a warm place to sit for an hour or so. Also, there were people to talk to and information of all kinds to be gleaned, from the latest mood of the authorities regarding permits right down to the more homely necessities of life. The cold and the unrelenting tension combined to make the perpetual tramping of the streets a matter of acute discomfort unless the whereabouts of every public convenience on his route were known. Kurt suspected that he was still suffering from the effects of his long drive into Belgium in the biting cold so that he could no longer risk an uncharted journey across Brussels. But even in this problem he was not alone: a fellow sufferer in his lunch group advised him to look for churches and plot his route accordingly. All churches, he pointed out, have at least one high wall, and are unfrequented and without windows. As Kurt thanked him gravely it occurred to him that steeplechasing had suddenly acquired a whole new meaning for him.

In a letter from home his father asked whether he remembered a family friend called Schinagl, whose brother lived in Brussels and had an office in the rue Fossé aux Loups. Kurt lost no time in calling on him, and although painfully conscious of his unwashed, unkempt appearance, his clothes betraying all too clearly that they performed night duty too, he found Herr Schinagl sympathetic and helpful. He could not, of course, offer Kurt employment without a work permit, but he extended a welcome to his visitor who came constantly to sit for an hour or more where it was warm, and talk of home. About this time he ran into another old acquaintance who had been a fellow member of The Austria, a rowing club in Vienna. He was a Czechoslovakian named Spitz, of Jewish origin, converted to Roman Catholicism and since turned atheist. His line of business was no less individual than this colourful character himself: he bought and sold human hair to be woven into a strong cloth. This was used for pressing sunflower seeds to extract the oil from them in the manufacture of margarine. At nearly seventy years old he was still a great ladies' man and loved to boast extravagantly of his latest conquests. Kurt had always liked him, and when he was invited to Herr Spitz's private hotel – roughly every other Sunday – it was not only the four-course lunch that made each occasion a red letter day.

He made some young friends too. One of these, also from Vienna, already had a visa for South America and was only waiting to emigrate. He warned Kurt that his shabby appearance could cause him to be picked up as a vagrant, spelling worse trouble for him. For a few memorable weeks he lent Kurt a coat which was smart and very thick. Then one day he managed to get his journey fixed up and he left Brussels, taking his lovely coat with him, while Kurt reverted sadly to his own. It was torn from constant wear and seemed thinner and shabbier than ever.

It was not until the middle of February that Kurt received the encouraging news that his trunk had arrived in Brussels. This he had been packed weeks before in Vienna with almost everything he possessed, for it was obvious that he would have no money for any new clothing during the foreseeable future. For one thing, no one was allowed to take more than 10 marks (about £1) out of the country, although Kurt had thought of a way round this when he dispatched the luggage. He knew it was no use hiding money in the trunk because this would have been discovered at the customs in Vienna when the contents were checked before the trunk was sealed and passed fit to go. Instead, he had arrived at the depot with a small handful of gold coins in his pocket. Alas, true to his upbringing, he had made such a superb job of packing that the customs officer had opened the trunk and exclaimed that it was far too tidy to disturb. He had closed it again and sealed it on the spot, without further examination, giving Kurt no opportunity of slipping the coins in while he repacked, as he had intended.

The trunk itself would make a most useful addition to his spartan attic. His father had bought it for him for the occasion, and when it was stood on end it formed a wardrobe fitted with coat hangers. To claim it now from the customs depot would cost about twice his weekly allowance, but the Jewish Committee made up the amount and also paid for a van to take it to the rue Brogniez. When it arrived he had to unpack in the hall and take everything upstairs an armful at a time, the stairs being too narrow to negotiate the trunk when full. As Kurt climbed up and down with each load his landlady looked on with admiration and ill-concealed amazement, for a textile business means good quality clothes. Ordinarily he would have been amused at the impression he was making as he caught sight of her surreptitiously fingering the Harris tweeds and eyeing his dinner jacket with a kind of awe. The thought of having a trunkful of clean, warm, respectable clothes had been an immense relief, and he had looked forward to unpacking his belongings with keen anticipation. In the event, however, the pleasurable excitement had been completely ruined for him, and his mind was in such a turmoil that he hardly noticed what he was carrying upstairs. To claim his trunk from the railway he had had to produce his passport, and without any warning or explanation, this had been confiscated.

He slept very little that night. Even the luxury of clean pyjamas covered by a soft woollen sweater did nothing to erase his memories of the last few weeks before he had left Vienna. One day in November 1938 he had received a sudden summons to attend a German military call-up depot. As a Jew, he could not join up, which suggested only deeply sinister reasons for calling him in. Any hopes he might have entertained that this was a mistake were shattered on his arrival. He was given a form with his name already on it and put in a room with a group of other young Jews, all of them as anxious as himself. Here they were told to strip naked and parade before a desk, where they were inspected, measured and weighed and eventually seen by a doctor who declared Kurt fit for military service. While he dressed again, his mind had been racing: was there going to be a war? If so, what job were they lining up for him, since he would not be eligible to fight? Whatever they were planning, he was now on their files, a known Jew at the mercy (or otherwise) of the German Army. They could, and would, justify anything they wanted to do with anyone, and as a Jew he had no rights whatsoever.

At home once more that night, after long discussion with his parents, it was decided that Kurt was now too vulnerable to remain in Vienna any longer. He had to get out of the country before it was too late. If he had been called in by the Germans once, it could certainly happen again, especially now that they had his name on the files. True to their roots in Judaism, his parents saw the future of the race invested in the next generation, and in their own case, in their only son. They did not feel themselves to be in any great danger yet, but Kurt, they insisted, must escape. They would hear no other point of view.

To get the necessary passport and papers to prove that he owed nothing in the way of taxes when he left meant many hours of waiting around outside the relevant offices, mostly in the company of other Jews who were equally anxious to get out before they were sent to concentration camps. These queues were intensely vulnerable to marauding Germans who would round them up on sight, after which they would be lucky if they got away with a beating. The Picks, like many others in the same situation, had employed a man who was prepared to accept payment for taking the risk of standing in this queue. This man, as in so many similar cases, had evidently been arrested, for he had never returned. The next day the police had arrived to order Kurt to report to the Gestapo Headquarters on the following day. His father had been alone in the house when the summons came, and he had lain awake all night keeping his hell to himself rather than distress his family a moment sooner than he need. Kurt, indeed, had remained ignorant of any anxiety until he had seen his father's ashen face and hollow eyes at breakfast, but his mother, who had witnessed her husband's restless thrashing, was frantic even before she knew the reason for his distress.

The sight of his parents that morning came back to haunt Kurt now. Lying awake on the narrow iron bed in the rue Brogniez, he shook with fear as well as cold as he recalled in vivid detail his summons to the infamous Hotel Metropole in the Morzin Platz. That this would be a deportation sentence not one of them had doubted. Kurt had telephoned a few close relatives and friends, given them a brief explanation and bidden them a goodbye that had meant precisely that. He had kissed his parents, the formality of his upbringing dissolving suddenly in an agonising upsurge of affection that he had always known existed but had rarely seen.

By the time he had reached the main reception desk he had already felt as though he were a criminal merely by his existence. Germans in every sort of uniform were in evidence, from those who wore brown shirts manning all the desks to high-ranking Nazis in black shirts whose word was instant law. He reported to the officer on duty and went through the inevitable formality of answering the questions on a form.

Then he was given a piece of paper which had to be returned bearing the signature of the official concerned before he would be allowed out of the building. He was in effect a prisoner already. From there he was sent upstairs to present himself in another office. At every turn, he felt hostile eyes upon him, conscious that he was prey to anyone who cared to stop him, whether to question him, beat him up or arrest him with a view to deportation. He felt trapped on the fifth floor of the building, even though he knew that on his return to the main hall his predicament would be no better. There was no escape until the piece of paper had been signed. He knocked at the door, his knees beginning to shake at the thought of what might happen when he was admitted.

He went in and explained to the German behind the desk that he wanted his passport. The German looked at him, studied the form Kurt gave him for a minute or two, handed him his passport, and then signed the all-important piece of paper. The man at the reception desk downstairs took the paper from Kurt, looked at it and said politely, 'Goodbye'. Kurt went straight to the nearest telephone kiosk and rang his parents with the incredible news that he was free.

The fact that he had walked out that day, reborn, into the Vienna sunshine, counted for nothing now, as he shivered in his attic. The ghost that had returned to keep him company this night was the same cold sweat of panic, the hollow nausea of dread.

He went to the Jewish Committee as soon as it opened next morning and told his story. Immediately, he was led into an inner office and interviewed by two or three higher-ranking officials than hitherto he had seen there. They listened with great concern, taking down the particulars in detail and discussing the possible implications with Kurt and among themselves. He learned that this had never happened before, so there was no guiding precedent; it might indeed be a new move by the authorities which could have an adverse effect on them all. After much deliberation it was decided that, in the current situation, Kurt had the right to demand the return of his passport. Greatly to his relief a social worker was provided to accompany him next day to the *Ministère de la Justice*. She was a young Belgian woman, probably Jewish, well spoken and well dressed. More than that, she would be officially recognised by those with whom he had to deal. Kurt warmed to her, deeply reassured by her manner and competence, the more so because she seemed genuinely interested in the plight of this very unusual client. She disappeared into the building to do all the negotiating on his behalf, and emerged after a while smiling, with Kurt's passport in one hand, and in the other a *feuille de route* valid for three months from 21 February.

Once again his luck had held.

Out of the blue Kurt received an invitation to dine with a professor of German literature at Brussels University. He arrived to find a charming house, a kind welcome and a delicious meal awaiting him – but no satisfactory answer to his question: who was responsible for this introduction? His host evaded giving a direct reply, indicating that somehow he had heard that Kurt had arrived without a visa and might be glad of hospitality, and then changed the subject with a finality which prevented his guest from probing further. Long afterwards, for various reasons, Kurt suspected the social worker who had retrieved his passport for him, but at the time he was content to receive with gratitude the kindness extended to him by this new friend.

There was no place for self-pity on such occasions, nor indeed was Kurt given to dwelling on the deprivations of his life, but the professor must have understood his situation and sensed his loneliness in a strange country. He acquired for Kurt admission to the university library, which was not only a warm place to sit unobtrusively for many hours on end, but was responsible for his proficiency in English, acquired through the books he read there. The library also provided a breath from home in the unlikely guise of the *Manchester Guardian*. In his own university days at the *Hochschule für Welthandel* in Vienna he had often bought a copy to take home on the tram, less for the sake of its content than because it completed the effect so earnestly desired by every fashionable young man of his day – that of the perfect English gentleman.

Now that he had regained confidence in his appearance, Kurt decided to renew acquaintance with the Sonntags on whose floor he had slept his first night in Brussels. He found them waiting to sail to South America, their young family already outgrowing the clothes their parents had bought them for the journey. Kurt had not only studied economics, he had also done a two-year tailoring course, and although he had never reached a professional standard he knew enough about it to repay the Sonntags' hospitality by altering the children's clothes for the voyage.

As he worked, he talked with the family. They spoke of their hopes of getting away to a new life, of the necessity for getting money out of their own country in order to prove some financial backing to the country of destination. Kurt told Herr Sonntag that his parents planned to take as much as possible to Italy and then to proceed by boat to Australia, while he himself hoped to go via England, since his father, who had connections with several British firms, had some money in Manchester. It was necessary to prove possession of at least £200 for admission to Australia, he said, and Herr Sonntag agreed that times were very hard, adding that it was a case of survival of the fittest. Kurt sighed and picked up another little pair of trousers; only later was he to remember those words with bitter clarity.

Herr Sonntag knew as well as Kurt that the Nazis were grabbing the possessions of all well-to-do Jews as they fled from Austria. If any of them owned a business, then a commissar was put in to handle the cash, and in the autumn of 1938 all Jewish bank accounts had been closed suddenly. Kurt remembered vividly the day this had happened: he had answered the telephone early in the morning to hear a voice in a call-box warning his family of this impending closure and urging them to withdraw their money immediately. The caller had remained anonymous, but Kurt had recognised the voice of the bank's *Generaldirektor*, Karl Weninger, who had risked his life alerting the Picks to their predicament. Kurt had been dispatched at once, arriving at the bank as the doors opened. He withdrew almost the whole of their account, and as he left, the cashiers had already been shutting the grilles behind him. Jewish people who had got wind of the situation only minutes after the Picks were being turned away with nothing.

There had still been a problem, of course. The Nazis could grab anything on the slightest pretext, and anyone witnessing Kurt's successful foray to the bank might have informed on him. After much thought Kurt's father had hidden the money under the top of the living-room table. It had no drawers to attract a search, but it did have a solid wooden support running round it above the legs, forming an interior shelf.

Every problem, like every conversation, came back to money in the end. Without money Kurt's parents could not leave Vienna; without money none of them could obtain a passage to Australia, and without a further £200 none of them would be allowed entry on arrival. Kurt confided to Herr Sonntag that he was having difficulty simply surviving, let alone trying to save a sum of such magnitude. Herr Sonntag asked him quietly whether his mother had any jewellery, suggesting that his parents must have some small valuables in Vienna. He reminded Kurt that couriers with diplomatic bags travelled between Belgium and Austria, unchecked by the customs. And as Kurt laid down his work and gave him his whole attention, Herr Sonntag added that he knew a way to help him which was safe and foolproof.

That evening Kurt returned to his attic with a headful of instructions. He took a sheet of paper and wrote to his father, making use of a pre-arranged code they had agreed in Vienna.

'I am writing this,' he began, 'on a wild, wet night.' A comment on the weather in the first sentence would prompt his father to look under the stamp. The beginnings of successive paragraphs would give a clue to whatever was written there.

'A friend of mine hopes to visit Vienna soon,' wrote Kurt, rubbing his fingers to maintain the circulation, for the draught was finding its way to him from every angle. Further down the page with another indentation he began again: 'They say the best things in life come in small packages...'

He hoped his father would read it more carefully than the censor; it was the strangest, as well as the dullest letter he had ever written home. When it was finished he sealed the envelope and then wrote in pencil in the top right hand corner, 'How much?' Over this he stuck the stamp.

During the following week he became progressively more certain that his father had either misunderstood or missed altogether the message hidden in the letter, so that when he received a reply it was with great trepidation that he hurried upstairs to read it.

'We have been having the same gales that you mention,' were the first words he read. With hands that trembled with excitement, Kurt brought out his electric beaker and when the water boiled he carefully peeled off the stamp in the steam. It concealed a figure in Austrian currency worth about £200. Kurt breathed deeply and toasted Herr Sonntag in horlicks while he read the rest of the news from home.

He visited the Sonntags again next day and at the first opportunity told his host that his father had agreed to take advantage of the proposed scheme. Herr Sonntag took a bank note of negligible value from his pocket and cut it in two with the tailoring scissors lying on the table between them. He replaced half the note in his pocket and gave the other half to Kurt.

This, he explained, was Kurt's counterfoil. He was to let his father know the number on it. The other piece went to the bank with his father's valuation of the goods. In return he would receive the bank's guarantee for that amount, as his security. When the courier called at his home he would present the bank's half to Alfred Pick, who had to check the number against the one Kurt had given him. If they were the same, his father should hand over the goods in return for the half bank note. Herr Sonntag would then claim them for Kurt from the bank by producing his half of the bank note plus the bank's guarantee and their commission. If anything went wrong, Alfred Pick must send Kurt his half, and on presentation of the two halves together with the guarantee, the bank would compensate him.

The next time they met, Herr Sonntag handed over a sheet of paper guaranteeing to Kurt the equivalent of £200 in the event of the loss of the valuables at any stage of the transaction. Kurt took out his pocket book and asked for the name and address of the bank, which did not appear on the paper. Herr Sonntag replied that the bank preferred to remain anonymous for security reasons. Kurt pointed out politely that he was acting on behalf of his father who would never accept as a guarantee such an unbusiness-like document. Herr Sonntag hesitated, and then conceded the point. With more than a little reluctance he gave Kurt the name of the bank and its address in Antwerp.

Any qualms Kurt might have had about the scheme proved quite unjustified. In a few weeks he received from Herr Sonntag, via an unseen chain of link-men, his mother's diamond brooch, a few gold coins and some other small items of jewellery and cash. He deposited them in a small safe at the Westminster Bank in the Place Royale, where he opened an account by virtue of a reference from Herr Schinagl. He derived immense satisfaction from calling there occasionally, dressed in his best English suit, to be greeted deferentially first by the doorman and then by the cashier from whom he requested access to his safe. In the privacy of the vault he would reassure himself of its contents, the whole of which he held in trust for his parents against their day of need.

Soon afterwards, Kurt heard from his father that Vienna was in the grip of a sudden cold spell. Upon removing the stamp and studying the letter, he learned that his Uncle Franz had been so much impressed by the success of his father's transaction that he wished to avail himself of the same facility, the only difference being that he had goods for collection to the tune of £1,000. Kurt had to hold his father's minute, precise writing close against the light bulb to read it at all, let alone decipher the message it contained, and being somewhat blasé about the whole procedure by now, he would have liked to suggest that another time it would save trouble if everything but the first sentence went under the stamp.

Herr Sonntag was willing again to act as go-between, and in a day or two the bank confirmed that they would guarantee the goods at the same rate as before. The cogs turned smoothly: Kurt hardly wondered how each stage was progressing until the time came to call upon the Sonntags and collect his uncle's valuables.

He sensed a difference as soon as he walked into the flat. To begin with, Frau Sonntag was in the throes of packing their possessions, having received notice that they would shortly be given berths on a ship to South America. Kurt was invited into a back room where he found Herr Sonntag with another man he had not seen before. He guessed that this was a link in the chain, and he guessed too that something had gone wrong.

Herr Sonntag came straight to the point. There was a problem, he said. The goods, consisting of a solid gold cigarette case and a diamond necklace, had been guaranteed for £1,000 had they not? Kurt assented. Herr Sonntag was apologetic, but the bank would not accept this figure; they had valued the things at quite a lot more. He turned to the link man who nodded and confirmed that it was thirty per cent more. Apparently there was no problem over the cigarette case, but the necklace – seventy stones set in platinum – was worth £330 more than had been declared. Herr Sonntag pointed out that consequently Kurt owed the bank the percentage on the difference before they would hand over the goods.

Kurt was flabbergasted. He insisted vehemently that it was impossible for his uncle to have been so mistaken. Eventually he agreed to the suggestion of an independent valuation, and accordingly, a few days later, they set out together to visit a jeweller recommended by Herr Sonntag. It was a little place near the Opera with an office upstairs where an old man greeted them from behind a desk. Herr Sonntag placed the necklace before the jeweller, asking him to give his opinion of its value. The old man scrutinised the diamonds and counted them. He examined the setting carefully and presently confirmed almost exactly the figure Herr Sonntag had mentioned. It was a conservative estimate, he said. Some of the stones were really very fine and it might even be worth rather more than that.

They returned to the Sonntags' flat in silence. Kurt had no option but to hand over the balance of the money in return for the cigarette case and the diamond necklace. He added both to his safe and went home to write to his father.

It would have been a difficult letter in any case: transposing it into the agreed code proved almost impossible. He found his inventive powers inhibited by the thought of the questions he was raising at home. He could hear the exact tone of his father's voice saying, 'Let us be perfectly clear about this: the jeweller who confirmed the valuation was a man of Herr Sonntag's choice, was he not?' Worse still, he could picture his uncle wrestling with a mounting suspicion that he, Kurt, had succumbed to the very human temptation of trumping up this story in order to obtain more money from home for himself.

Finally, he began to ask his own questions. Herr Sonntag had talked about survival of the fittest; he was about to emigrate with his family and would need every penny he could scrape together. It was only a short step further for Kurt to start wondering: if the bank had not been prepared to hand over the goods on the receipt of the original commission, how was it they had parted with them for an independent valuation? He sat thinking for a long time, and then, his hands grown white with cold, he crumpled the half-written letter and went out again.

Herr Schinagl was still in his office. He greeted Kurt with surprise and listened gravely to all he had to say. At the end he nodded several times and then asked if Kurt knew of a jeweller of his own selection. Kurt remembered meeting a neighbour of the Sonntags who was a Flemish diamond merchant. He was a hard-looking man with humourless, steel-blue eyes, but there was no reason to suppose him any less honest for that.

Kurt waited until dusk to make his call, anxious that none of the Sonntags should catch sight of him there. The visit only lasted ten minutes; he left with the name and address of a well-known jeweller where he was to meet the Flemish dealer next morning. He arrived to find better class premises this time with quality goods on view beneath the glass topped counters. After a brief introduction he produced the necklace, explaining that he had been quoted two figures and would like to know which valuation was correct. The jeweller inspected the diamonds: the necklace was a good one, he assured Kurt, but he was sorry, he himself would place its value at a little less than the lower figure mentioned.

Kurt turned up at Herr Schinagl's office that afternoon breathing fire and smoke against Herr Sonntag and the link man. Herr Schinagl was deeply sympathetic but pointed out that if confronted, they would only blame the bank. He advised Kurt that he must have proof before he started accusing anyone, otherwise he would only end up in the wrong himself.

Kurt knew this to be true; fortunately, he also knew which bank it was. Facing up to the possibility of existing on half rations of bread and milk for a week, he took a train to Antwerp immediately and walked to the address he had been given. The next part was not so easy: he had no idea for whom to ask, let alone how to explain what he wanted. The cashier seemed determined not to understand what Kurt was talking about, and it was only when the facts began to be embarrassingly plain in front of the other clients that Kurt was shown into an office in order to be heard in private. The bank official who came to speak to him blanched at the realisation that Kurt had been able to discover which bank was involved, but he turned grey with horror at the denouement of Kurt's story. Trembling, he affirmed that the original valuation for the necklace was the correct one. Then he hurried Kurt out of the building as if his very presence could bring ignominy and ruin upon the establishment.

When confronted, Herr Sonntag was taken so much by surprise that he broke down in tears and confessed to everything, more to Kurt's disgust than satisfaction. He became less abject, however, when Kurt demanded his money back, and pointed out that the link man was just as culpable. Eventually they agreed on a conference, with Herr Schinagl present on Kurt's insistence.

It was a stormy meeting. The link man was sullen and intractable, and became abusive when Kurt spoke of a swindle. It was Kurt, he shouted, who had committed the treachery in betraying their confidence by going to the bank. In destroying this trust he had destroyed the link man's livelihood, and far from receiving any money, Kurt should be made to pay compensation. Herr Schinagl tried valiantly to intervene, backing

Kurt, but his words were drowned by the link man's livid threats to denounce Kurt to the Jewish Committee for not declaring the valuables he kept in the bank. In the end Herr Sonntag accepted responsibility for his half of the amount owed, and promised to have the money ready for Kurt in a couple of days. The link man, however, snorted that Kurt would not get a penny piece out of him after the way he had been treated.

'In that case,' Kurt told him, 'I certainly do owe you something, and I propose to give it to you now'. And with all the force at his command he punched the link man on the nose.

Two days later he went round to collect Herr Sonntag's debt. There was an unnatural silence on the stairs and he found the door of the flat ajar. He pushed it open and went in, his footsteps echoing on the empty boards from which every stick of furniture had been removed. Herr Sonntag and his family had gone.

Herr Spitz had also sustained a sudden loss, and he sought Kurt's company for consolation. The favoured lady of the moment – a secretary in his office – had just quit her job, leaving him distraught. Would Kurt care to celebrate his seventieth birthday with him? Kurt, equally in need of cheering, accepted with pleasure, and a few days later made his way to a coffee house near the Opera, in the Place de la Monnaie.

His host greeted him extravagantly and ordered a supper to match. It was to be just the two of them, Herr Spitz having quarrelled with everyone else he knew, even his son. The fault, of course, lay with the late lamented secretary for leaving him. Herr Spitz's voice began to rise indignantly at the way he had been treated, but he described the charms of the absent lady to Kurt while they waited for champagne to be brought to the table. She was, he confided over the foie gras, utterly fascinating, adding, as all conversation ceased at the six nearest tables, that she could sit on her hair – her beautiful golden tresses, the colour of the wine they were drinking! He held up his glass to the light and gave a groan which turned heads several tables away, while Kurt tried to steer the subject along different lines.

Herr Spitz bit savagely into a rare fillet steak that dissolved at the merest touch, while the atmosphere grew warm and rich. Behind the mountain of French fried potatoes between them, Kurt was beginning to find it hard to concentrate. Another cork popped: they drank to Herr Spitz and many more happy returns; they drank to all those who preferred parties to squabbling; they even drank to secretaries everywhere who sat on their golden hair.

Hours later they emerged slowly into the lighted street. The air was mild and moist, and as Kurt let himself in through the front door in the rue Brogniez he felt replete and comforted, at peace with all the world. There was a postcard waiting for him in the dim little hallway; he focused on it with difficulty, presently recognising the scrawl as his mother's writing. The message was very short and he had to read it twice before he took in its meaning.

His father had been arrested.

He walked. He had no destination, just a cold grey emptiness in the pit of his stomach. The rest of him was disembodied, floating a little above the young man who walked the streets shivering in the aftermath of the night before. He watched the familiar shoes moving alternately one ahead of the other, but had no power to direct their progress or quicken their pace. Outside Sarma's Stores he started across the road, glancing to the right as if he were still in pre-Nazi Vienna. There was a sudden screech and the angry blast of a motor horn. Instinctively, Kurt dived for the safety of the kerb, the acrid smell of scorched rubber filling his nostrils, the driver's furious swearing in his ears.

For a while he remained sitting there, shaking at the near miss. Then he stood up, dusting his trousers, and continued on his pointless walk to nowhere. It occurred to him that had he been killed, a crowd would have gathered and someone would have had to dispose of his remains. But not a soul in the world would ever have heard what had happened to him.

Kurt Pick would have simply disappeared.

PART II

Marneffe and Brussels

CHAPTER 3

June 1939-May 1940

He came to the Château of Marneffe on a fine morning in the middle of June. By the time the two buses had passed through the village and were continuing up the slight incline, leaving a deep valley falling away below, the sun was already making the seats sticky to the touch. Kurt would gladly have stripped off his pullover, but sitting at such close quarters there was no room for manoeuvre, especially with a typewriter pressing into his knees. All the same, the sunshine was a welcome experience after the long, bitter winter – as much a new beginning as the adventure ahead of him – and he was grateful for the chance of this job, however temporary it proved to be.

Kurt had met at Herr Schinagl's office in Brussels a young man called Walter whom he had tried to help find somewhere to live, until Walter had announced that he had found a much nicer room than Kurt's attic in the rue Brogniez – and in a much better part of town. Kurt, somewhat nettled by this, had turned green with envy when he heard that the room was on the ground floor right next to a bistro. And it was run, Walter had pointed out smugly, by such very charming people.

He had moved in the same day while Kurt in his icy crowsnest gnashed his teeth with jealousy. Next morning, however, Walter had been round at first light, banging on Kurt's door. He had invited in his charming hosts to find himself surrounded by a crowd of homosexuals. His alarm was not the blind prejudice it might be supposed nowadays: such practices were illegal at that time, and consequently highly dangerous. The doorman, apparently, had a warning button by his foot to press if the police came, but to Kurt's unconcealed delight, Walter had discovered with horrified indignation that there was not even a lock on the door.

Walter, it had to be admitted, had had the last laugh. Shortly afterwards much milder weather had arrived and Kurt had been the one to find himself invaded by undesirable neighbours. His mattress had begun to heave with bed bugs waking out of hibernation. When he had complained to his landlady her only surprise had been his reaction, as she assured him ingenuously that they were even to be found in her daughter's room.

As a result of all this, Kurt and Walter had become great friends and had moved into rooms in the same house near the Stock Exchange, and when Walter got a job with the Jewish Committee he had promised to keep an eye open for something for Kurt.

The number of refugees at that time in Brussels and Antwerp was creating problems for the police, and the Belgian Government had either to tighten up on restrictions or provide camps to accommodate them. There was already a camp for young men; now plans were afoot to start one for families in an empty château which had been a Jesuit school. This was to be financed mainly by the International Jewish Joint Committee, subsidised by the Government, and was to be entirely self-sufficient.

Walter called in on Kurt one evening and told him that in a few days' time a party of tradesmen was to set off to prepare the place and render it habitable. Someone was needed to go

for a few weeks in an administrative capacity to act as interpreter and co-ordinator. Perhaps, suggested Walter, Kurt
might like the job?

They arrived at an imposing gateway with a lodge from which
the caretaker, M Bis, came out to admit them. Kurt, in the second bus, could see glimpses of a park through a wrought-iron
fence above which rose copper beech trees and chestnuts,
their pink and white candles in full flower. He caught the
scent of honeysuckle as the gates swung open and the whole
company passed through. Wood pigeons called to each other,
and on either side of the drive there was a scarlet splash of
poppies in the lush, midsummer grass.

When the buses came to a halt in front of the house the
passengers filed out and mingled in little groups, their bags in
their hands, waiting for M Bis to unlock the door. Kurt found
himself standing beside a short, stocky man with an impish
face and the muscles of a boxer, whose eyes sized everyone
up with undisguised impertinence. He stepped forward and
offered Kurt a hand several sizes too large for its owner, with
a grip to match.

'Mandler,' he said briefly.

'Pick,' replied Kurt – and Pick he remained to everyone
throughout the whole of his time at Marneffe.

They walked up a dozen stone steps, past fluted columns,
into a marble hall from which two wide staircases curved
upwards, one on either side, between ornate, wrought-iron
balustrades. Dwarfed by the cool austerity of the building,
they tiptoed after the caretaker: on the right was a 40-foot
panelled drawing-room, on the left an even longer banqueting
hall, connecting at the end with another, smaller hall and
staircase. M Bis opened each door leading off this in turn,
revealing several smaller rooms. Kurt put down the typewriter in one of these and flexed his arms with relief. Here,
he decided, with its fine view of the grounds and greater
degree of intimacy, he would have his office.

The first floor was arranged in suites, and above this were about 25 single bedrooms, in one of which Kurt staked out another claim. Not all the accommodation was in the château: a long cloister had been added round an open quadrangle linking the main house to other buildings in which had lived the Jesuit community and its pupils. Beyond this was the park; still further, trees had been planted in formal avenues, their perspective giving the deliberate impression that the grounds extended further than they did. The end of each walk met with a high iron fence forming a continuous boundary between the estate and the world outside.

Those inside were essentially pioneers. They consisted of skilled cooks, plumbers, electricians, carpenters etc, the very emptiness of the place presenting a challenge to their various resources. Materially, they started from scratch, but the rich assets of occupation, a purpose in life and security for the next few weeks were beyond price.

Kurt found himself busier than he had ever been. He was in charge of the catering, ordering not only food but all the tools and materials needed for the work to be carried out. Even before he had left Brussels the pressure of increasing numbers of refugees had been steadily building, since the government, like its Dutch counterpart, persisted in a humane policy towards potential victims of Nazi persecution. Several refugee camps had been formed to take the heat off the Jewish immigrants themselves and also the authorities who were coping with the problems they created. The rush was on to provide places and to fill them, with a deadline to be met on both sides of the fence. Within a week, work on the first section of rooms was well enough advanced to estimate a date for receiving the first refugees.

At this point the weather broke. The wind tore across the park driving the heavy summer rain against the empty buildings and blotting out the hills. Kurt woke in the night to the smell of soaking earth and the sound of windows being shut. Then there were urgent voices and running footsteps down the long corridor outside his room. He opened his door and saw that the cause of the disturbance had been a dark stain on the ceiling. It spread as he watched it and water began to pour through a crack in the middle with the speed of a fully open tap. Buckets had to be placed in strategic positions all over the top floor, with people whose rooms were affected moving in on more fortunate neighbours.

In a few days summer returned, but the roof of the main building had become a priority. All other work ceased while repairs were effected, and the arrival date for the first batch of residents was put back. The workmen talked of the delay in returning to their families, making Kurt realise with a jolt his total involvement in the place.

The flood did not prevent the arrival about a week later of Michel Matton to take up the post of Director at Marneffe. He was a Flemish civil servant, a prison governor, a tall, spare man with a tightly-buttoned face and an inscrutable manner, who inspired the whole range of respect from loyalty to awe in his subordinates. If his temper was somewhat unpredictable – due in part to the apparent stiffness of his facial muscles which gave no clue to his mood – his integrity was undoubted and his word was law. His was no desk job but a deeply personal commitment to everyone at the camp, and he made himself endlessly available to listen to people and to appreciate their problems. It was his habit to seek out Kurt first thing every morning to shake him by the hand, and this would be accompanied by a wink which Kurt had come to expect as part of an informal greeting from all Belgians. If Matton omitted this ceremony something was wrong, and Kurt would start to wonder what he had done to upset him.

Later, Mme Matton moved in with her husband as uncrowned queen of Marneffe. She was also Flemish and the very correct French she had learnt to speak created a much more aristocratic impression than she deserved. She had a high opinion of her own position as her husband's consort, and soon established herself at the top of the pecking order, with the help of a thin veneer of charm which was just enough to dazzle those she patronised into an obsequious submission.

Matton brought two men with him: a Flemish technical officer called Verbist and a clerical officer. The latter was a pathetic, frightened little man who was terrified of his own wife as well as Matton. He was supposed to deal with all the correspondence but it soon became evident that he had no idea even how to set out a letter. A strange partnership developed between him and Kurt, who could hardly speak the language but had learnt enough commercial French to do the job for him. Kurt found him an odd creature, very narrow and bigoted in his outlook, with deeply prejudiced views.

Life was too busy, however, what with the bulk buying, studying catalogues of unfamiliar things and then ordering them in French, not to mention the secretarial work which Matton now handed over to him – to give more than a passing thought to the way the clerk followed him round and watched him. Only in retrospect did he notice this attention, and by then he had cause enough to know the reason for it.

When the families began to arrive some of the workmen chose to stay and were joined by their wives and children. Matton came to Kurt's room, shook hands and then paced the floor in silence for a moment. Suddenly he turned to him and said, 'I could use you. Do you want to stay?'

Kurt hardly knew how to answer him. He belonged there; it was *his* Marneffe. It had never occurred to him to leave.

The office Kurt had chosen was nothing like big enough now for the growing administration, and Matton moved him into what had once been the banqueting hall. This became the Office, the hub of management, so that a desk here was a status symbol, lending the user an aura of importance quite out of proportion to the job he did there. Soon, a further snobbery evolved: that of the position of each desk. It was deemed grander to sit at Kurt's end of the hall, the newer desks having been added to the other end. A hierarchy developed and places were jealously annexed and then guarded, the resulting politics ending inevitably in squabbles and resentment. At last a pompous young man made a scene at being given a desk in a 'low' position. Kurt, finally exasperated with them all, offered to swap with him, installing himself at the humble end of the room. For an hour or so everyone was happy; then Matton came in to discuss something of immediate importance with Kurt – who was of course missing. The ensuing fireworks promptly produced a return to the original arrangement.

If the Office caused problems, they were nothing to those created by the plumbing. Mandler had declared war on it within 24 hours of his arrival, plunging into manholes and bullying it into submission with a zeal that wrung praise even from the usually reserved Matton. Mandler's enjoyment of the limelight extended to the length of the beam of Matton's torch directed down the steep, black sides of the pit as he indulged in hair-raising acrobatics to win a trickle of water for an admiring audience at ground level. But the root of the trouble was incurable, even for Mandler: it was an antiquated, inefficient system with a totally inadequate pressure for the amount of water required. For the first few weeks there was a bath rota, but once the residents began to arrive in any number – building to a full quota of 600 by October – this became unworkable. Nevertheless, all things are relative, and to Kurt, after the winter months of icy washing, a jug of hot water collected from the kitchen was luxury indeed.

Inevitably, the worst happened, and after a short time the lavatories became blocked. Something drastic had to be done, and since everyone living there had to be occupied in some way, two or three men were offered a small bonus to work the plunger. It was a truly terrible job, not only for all the obvious reasons but because of the social stigma attached to it. They became untouchables; their fellows shunned them for stinking and Kurt was bound to admit some truth in the accusation. Sadly, their wives suffered for the same reasons, and anyone who noticed these families at all witnessed first the disintegration of the men themselves and then the break up of their marriages. They were the first helpless casualties of overcrowding.

Hardly higher in some people's estimation came Obler, who worked in the laundry. His was another dirty job, back-breaking in the steam and requiring brute strength to manhandle the washing in and out of the vast industrial machines. Obler was as primitive as the work he did – a violent ruffian about whom there were forever complaints from those who crossed him. But he was efficient in his work, and extremely knowledgeable professionally, taking a special interest in Kurt's laundry which he insisted on doing by hand. Such fine materials, he said, must not be allowed near that ruinous machine. His manner was as ingratiating as the oily wheels that turned the huge drums, and Kurt knew it was largely his own status which prompted this special favour.

There were complaints about Mandler, too, but of a different kind. He was joined at Marneffe by his young wife and baby boy, of whom he was inordinately proud, although his eye continued to rove unchecked. His own attraction to women made matters worse: he was immensely strong, with boundless self-confidence and an unassailable line in one-upmanship. His lusty appetite for life was quite insatiable and some of the men cordially detested him for his cock-of-the-walk insistence on being at the centre of everything. Kurt, who had no axe to grind, dismissed it all as showing off, and they enjoyed a mutual respect for one another's ability.

Both of them held key positions on the staff, as it were, with all the attendant job satisfaction, plus a good deal of favour from Matton, but for most of the residents life was rather too much like a cross between a boarding school and a prisoner of war camp. The routine became irksome, the same people being allocated the same jobs week after week, and because no one ever moved on there were no prospects of promotion. The women felt the monotony most keenly: in this pre-war man's world they did only the 'feminine' chores of caring for their children, cleaning, serving and mending, all the creative jobs being by tradition men's work. There were also restrictions to be observed, not only on tangible things, particularly water, but on freedom. No one was allowed outside the confines of the grounds, one of the conditions of the setting up of the camp being that it kept itself to itself. Some people felt this more acutely than others; one elderly couple longed more than anything to break out of their cramped enclosure just once in a while, to do nothing more daring than a little expedition to the village. They wheedled Kurt, who was sorely tempted to indulge such an innocent whim, but had to refuse or the flood gates would have opened.

On the whole morale was high, although there were inevitably patches of discontent. These nearly always started with the wives, who had less to occupy them and less interesting work. The trouble would spill over to upset the husbands, sometimes gathering enough momentum to destroy the marriage. There was squabbling over the pecking order when jealousy was aroused over a husband's job, a position in the office or a coveted bedroom at the top of the main building. Every problem was aggravated by the lack of privacy: even at night couples found their married lives inhibited by the plywood-thin partitioning. Some resorted to running the taps to drown any sound until this became such a well-known ruse that it served rather to advertise what it sought to conceal. There was a sad toll of marital casualties, including a sorry little band of wife-swappers who simply never came to terms with the strict boundaries imposed by this confined life.

Matton was as flexible as possible. He did his best to provide what he could by way of entertainment: there was ping-pong, a canteen with a piano, and for the younger men football played vigorously on the open ground beyond the quadrangle. He was also tireless in his efforts to introduce different menus to suit all tastes, a thankless task with so many cultures and nationalities represented. There could be no question of orthodox food; even so, everyone wanted what he personally was used to, and most people grumbled that everything else was inedible. In spite of all that was done to make life pleasanter, it was still in many ways like being in prison, and the knowledge that Matton, with his pursed mouth and reserved manner, had been a prison governor did nothing to soften this impression. When once in a while he slipped up and referred to the residents as inmates, Kurt felt quite hurt at the allusion.

In spite of the fact that there were no new births at Marneffe, there were still a couple of hundred children at the camp by the time it had been open two months, most of them of an age to need full-time education. A school was started and Matton made the two hour journey to Brussels, coming back with an attractive twenty-year-old tomboy to take charge of the children's physical training. She was a qualified physiotherapist, half Jewish and with excellent French, so that the children, who adored her, soon became bilingual, playing games and learning PE in both French and German. Her name was Madeleine Weil but she was nicknamed Mouchie because her mother thought its Chinese flavour suited her dark hair and slightly almond eyes. Her enthusiasm was as charming as it was infectious and before Kurt had even set eyes on her, Matton took him to one side wagging a teasing finger, although his pale, expressionless face was as serious as ever.

'Be careful, Pick,' he warned.

Kurt was furious, all the more so when he found that the cap fitted perfectly.

The weeks that followed were among the most fulfilling he had ever known. Anything life lacked in creature comforts was amply compensated by comparison with the miseries of Brussels. Above all, he enjoyed the company he had longed for back in the lonely winter months. Part of his job was to interview all new arrivals and place them in accommodation and work where they would slot in most easily, enabling him to get to know and value many of the residents. But it is not possible to have more than a few close friends at a time, and small groups of kindred spirits soon gathered throughout the camp. Kurt and Mouchie, drawn immediately to each other, became part of an inner circle of six, the others being a dentist and his wife and another couple who were both doctors.

The dentist, Herr Meyerhardt, was an up-and-coming German with an elegant young wife. If they were, perhaps, inclined to dwell on the success and status they had achieved through having arrived in the best circles in Berlin, their friends readily overlooked it. Manners and taste were at a premium at Marneffe, and when the Meyerhardts talked a little grandly Kurt and Mouchie found it rather entertaining and politely hid their amusement.

The Halberstamms, on the other hand, were genuinely impressed that such a fine pair should condescend to them so kindly. They were Viennese but of Polish extraction, full of a strong Jewish family feeling, overflowing with the warmth of real compassion. Their love for their thirteen year old daughter had persuaded them to leave her with an aunt in Antwerp rather than bring her to a refugee camp, and they ached for her continuously. There were two other doctors at Marneffe, but Kurt noticed that it was the Halberstamms' golden-hearted caring that attracted most of the patients.

The two couples had been drawn together in the first place by their common medical interest, but a genuine friendship quickly developed between the six. There was little enough leisure for any of them until about nine o'clock each evening, when a magic hour of relaxation and sociability could be snatched before lights out.

Only one thing marred Kurt's happiness at this time, and that was concern for his parents, particularly since his father's arrest. He discussed it with his friends and with Matton. It was a measure of the latter's caring that he made time to listen to family problems however far removed from Marneffe. He heard Kurt attentively and then unearthed from the bottom of a drawer some headed writing paper. Kurt, reading the print from where he sat, could just make out that it was the official paper of the jail Matton had governed. Ten minutes later, Matton showed him the letter he proposed to send to the Governor of the prison in Vienna. It was a personal note from one colleague to another, mentioning Kurt as a valued member of his staff and enquiring for news of his father. Shortly afterwards, Alfred Pick was released.

Kurt was deeply appreciative of Matton's compassion and courage in sticking his neck out thus; nor did his efforts stop there. Kurt began to receive letters from home telling of harassment of his parents and their increasing fear of deportation. Vivid memories of his own life just before leaving Vienna left him in no doubt about the sort of thing they were suffering. He remembered tripping on a raised paving stone one day while running for the tram. A window had opened and a row of jeering faces had leaned out to laugh at the Jew boy sprawling on the ground. He had been lucky: others had been forced to scrub painted slogans off the pavements, using acid that burnt into their hands and clothes. He himself had been press-ganged on one occasion into cleaning a flat occupied by half a dozen Nazis. The thought of such things happening to his gentle, defenceless parents aroused in him feelings almost of panic. He confided to Matton that his parents were now desperate to get out of the country.

The result was a further official paper certifying that application had been made for visas to allow Kurt's parents entry into Belgium. Everything, it said, that should be done was in process of being dealt with, above board and in the approved fashion. Kurt knew that in itself the document was worthless, but its official character might render it quite invaluable in staving off further imprisonment or even deportation. Matton wrote out two of these, one for the Picks and one for Mandler to send to his parents, who were in a similar position.

Strangely, considerable risks like that did not appear to frighten Matton as much as official visits from prison inspectors and representatives of such bodies as the International Jewish Joint Committee. Sometimes he entertained them in small groups, more than a little concerned about his responsibility for the impression they received, although Marneffe became a showcase of efficiency. One of the highlights of Kurt's time there was the first occasion when Sir Herbert Emerson (later Lord Emerson), High Commissioner of Refugees to the League of Nations, visited Marneffe. He saw everything, including a performance by the children, who also sang the Belgian National Anthem. He even tasted the *potage du jour* while touring the kitchens, and keeping a stiff upper lip pronounced it delicious. Altogether the day was a huge success and everyone felt a personal pride in belonging there.

Visitors of this kind were not Kurt's only contact with life beyond the fence. It was his job to be the go-between with the local farmers who supplied Marneffe with produce. Twice that winter he set out in thick snow and, suddenly homesick for his native Austria, he managed to borrow a pair of skis and spent a blissful few hours being towed behind the van. There was a bit of envy and some not unpleasant ribbing from the others, especially during the second snowfall when he acquired another pair of skis and further enhanced his enjoyment by taking Mouchie with him.

As the catering increased to unmanageable proportions Matton took on a full-time buyer, while Kurt became the official link with the outside world, representing the camp and its interests. After a couple of months some people's passports had expired and Kurt, charged with the personal shopping lists of several residents, had the job of renewing 20 or so at a time at the German Consulate in Liège. He enjoyed these outings with their change of scenery and welcome sense of freedom. At the Consulate he was always greeted very correctly and once he was presented to the Vice-Consul, but at the same time he was conscious of a certain curiosity on the part of those who dealt with him, almost an attempt to discover more from him than their questions actually demanded. He always answered politely and established a cordial enough relationship, but whenever he was asked for further information, particularly concerning the whereabouts of anyone who had left the camp, he replied automatically that he did not know.

While he was waiting for the passports to be renewed Kurt would chat with the officials in a back room. On one occasion he found himself alone while a partly audible conversation was in progress in the next room. He could hear enough to arouse his interest and presently learned that the Vice-Consul was in contact with a Nazi in one of the border towns near Liège. This was a German town that had been retained by Belgium after the First World War and would therefore contain a strong Fifth Column. He realised he had been eavesdropping on some highly illegal business concerning the German underground movement, and on his return to Marneffe he told Matton of it in the strictest confidence.

The result surprised him. Matton came back to him two or three times for more information, and one day two strangers arrived from Brussels. They kept a very low profile and questioned Kurt closely in private. As he talked with them it dawned upon him that he had stumbled on counter-espionage activities of far greater importance than he had imagined at first.

Much later, Matton confided in him that no one ever managed to locate the Vice-Consul's contact. Kurt had formed the impression that the man was a teacher, but all enquiries had come to nothing. There could, he realised, have been Fifth Column infiltration at any stage of proceedings – even at Marneffe. Much later still he discovered to his cost that he was not the only one to wonder about that.

The outbreak of war on 3 September 1939 was not immediately of much concern to the residents of Marneffe. Their insular life was contained reassuringly within the greater boundaries of Belgium and Holland, which were still neutral, and together shielded them from hostilities. Any anxiety was quelled by Matton, who possessed the only wireless on the premises. He used to listen to the news in Flemish and feed encouragement to those who asked for information. Through him was filtered the fact that the Belgians had a hundred per cent confidence in the myth that the Albert Canal fortification (their continuation of the Maginot Line) was impregnable. It would, they were told, effectively prevent invasion, but even in the incredibly unlikely event of it falling, contingency plans would be put into operation, such as a train laid on to take them all to France.

One day at the end of April 1940, with life still very much as usual at Marneffe, Kurt walked to the village, taking a short cut on the return journey along the side of the cemetery. He was wearing a light-coloured raincoat against the frequent spring showers. The sudden drone of engines drew his attention to several low-flying aircraft coming towards him in formation. He had a fine view of them; only afterwards did he realise that they had an equally fine one of him. They were Belgian planes and as they approached, one of them broke away and dived straight at him, peppering the cemetery with sacks that exploded with a thud, scattering white powder at the point of impact. As Kurt continued to stand there, staring in amazement, one of the bombs landed almost at his feet, covering him with its contents, so that he looked exactly as if he had fallen into a flour barrel.

It was all over as suddenly as it had begun. Kurt hurried back to the camp in a great state of excitement to present himself to Matton, who got on the telephone at once. The incident was discussed exhaustively among the six friends for the rest of the evening, but by nightfall no one was any the wiser.

At six o'clock next morning Kurt was woken by the sound of gunfire. Running to the window he found he was on the wrong side of the house, so he hurried across the passage and burst unceremoniously into Mouchie's room. She was already out of bed and pointed excitedly almost directly overhead. The dogfight in progress was too high for the markings on either plane to be visible, but they could see the little puffs of gunfire and hear the sharp crack of each explosion.

People were downstairs to breakfast early that morning and when Kurt saw Mouchie again rumours were already flying. It had been taken for granted that one of the planes had been German; someone announced that Belgium had been attacked. Someone else came up with a message for Mouchie from Matton: Verbist was going to Brussels; she was to pack immediately and take a lift home with him. Kurt, wrenched between dismay and concern for her safety, hardly had time to say goodbye to her.

When Matton himself appeared at ten o'clock a sudden hush fell. Belgium, he told them gravely, was at war. Then, as an uproar broke out, he raised his hand for silence, and as soon as some semblance of quiet had been restored, he announced that everything was all right, the contingency plans would be put into action and meanwhile he would continue to keep them all informed.

For a day or two life returned to normal with no further excitements, and the panic retreated a little. But there was still great cause for anxiety: the road beyond the camp was a quiet rural lane with practically no traffic as a rule. Now, each morning began with the sight of a trickle of refugees tramping past the gate with such of their possessions as they could take with them. Kurt and his friends observed this, and although they said nothing to each other, they wondered what it might portend.

On 11 May the news suddenly grew worse. There were rumours that Liège had fallen, people began to urge evacuation from the camp and there was frantic speculation as to how soon the Germans might reach Marneffe. There was even talk of suicide, especially from those who had left Germany illegally and saw no prospect other than a concentration camp. Matton denied that he was perturbed, but Kurt noticed that he hardly left the telephone all day.

The following morning the road was jammed with refugees. They travelled with carts and trailers piled high with boxes and bundles of every description, and the procession showed no let-up all day. Such news as Matton could glean was far from encouraging, and even that came to an abrupt end after dark with a total blackout throughout the camp. Kurt and Mandler, Matton's two right-hand men, stayed up the whole night with him to be available in any emergency.

They sat in the hall in the dark, shivering because the silence was eerie and the air felt chilly with foreboding. Then, from far away, Kurt heard the throbbing of an engine. He stiffened, listening intently, aware that the others with him began to hear it too, until all three were leaning forward in their seats as the drumming grew louder and nearer. Eventually a Belgian military dispatch rider pulled up at the front door, the noise of his machine in the surrounding silence magnified into a mechanised regiment. He had lost his way. They were left again in the emptiness of the night.

The anticlimax served to galvanise Matton into hectic activity. Among other things he ordered evacuation papers to be typed immediately for everyone in the camp. Then, at first light, a platoon of Belgian soldiers arrived and surrounded the whole place, decreeing that all the residents were Germans and no one was allowed to leave the building.

Communication with the outside world had finally broken down, completely nullifying any contingency plans there may have been. Matton, at his courageous best in a crisis, became the captain who refused to leave his ship. Most probably he could have saved his own skin, leaving everyone else to sink or swim as they were able. Instead, he made a firm decision. Not for the first time, he pulled rank in the interests of those for whom he was responsible. His decision stood, with the result that the order was given for the camp to be evacuated.

There followed a period of frantic emergency packing, with everyone giving and getting advice on what should be taken and what left behind. Luggage that could not be carried was sealed and had to be abandoned in the cellars of the château. Kurt, having supervised the labelling and documenting of these possessions, saw to the issuing of the evacuation papers. He himself then dressed for warmth in a thick, white polo-necked sweater, the pale raincoat and strong ski boots, packing as much else as possible into a rucksack and a suitcase.

In all the turmoil and fear his last memories of Marneffe were unexpectedly dominated by a consuming, sickening pain. He was thankful to have Dr Halberstamm present to remove a long sharp splinter which had become detached from a floor board while he was packing and embedded itself excruciatingly underneath his fingernail.

Matton had driven on ahead with Verbist in the van, in order to try to make arrangements for the night. At his behest Kurt brought up the rear, and between them the 600 residents of Marneffe filed out to join the Belgian refugees already on the road. The Halberstamms and the Meyerhardts stayed at the back with Kurt – and so also, he noticed, did the clerk, who did not speak to him but was never more than a few yards from his side. They spilled into the main Huy to Namur road, another tributary to the swarming river of terrified humanity, and were swept round to the right with the current to head for France.

As they emerged from the Marneffe road an aeroplane appeared, flying very low above them. Herr Meyerhardt and Dr Halberstamm immediately grabbed their wives and pulled them into the ditch and then tackled Kurt in the same way, bending him almost double in the process. The plane passed over with a strange whistling sound and Kurt, overcome by curiosity, looked up to see the bomb dropping from it; as he ducked again it exploded in a field. They felt no blast or injury; there was just the sudden silence of shock. The comfortable insulation from hostilities was over: they were right in the middle of the horrors of war.

Minutes later they came to a cluster of houses round a farmyard where there were two or three carts piled with luggage. People were sitting in the carts as if waiting for imminent departure, but the horse between the shafts of one of them was lying on the ground. It seemed to Kurt that there was something strange about the way the driver slumped over the reins, and his horse, too, was motionless, without a flick of its tail against the flies. He looked again and the figures were all so very still, ghastly pale, their open eyes unblinking. He held onto his swimming senses by counting the corpses in this grisly tableau; eleven men, women and children, none of them with any sign of injury. They had all been killed instantly by the blast from the bomb.

On the opposite side of the road an elderly couple were tending a young girl who seemed from Kurt's brief glance to be unlikely to survive. The distress of all three was too painful to linger over, and he hurried past with the crowd.

Frau Halberstamm turned to him in disbelief. 'They are bombing refugees!' she said.

Her words jolted Kurt back to reality. If it had happened once it would no doubt happen again, and while they continued with the rest they were an easy target for the next attack. Beyond the houses a lane led off to the right, and this he took to see if he could find another way. He was disappointed: after a hundred yards the lane dwindled to a muddy footpath and came to an end in a field. He turned to find the clerk had come up behind him and now stood watching, his hands in his pockets.

'I thought we might have avoided the main road this way,' Kurt explained to him.

He returned to his friends and walked on again. The crowd was more strung out now and the five of them continued alone, for the little clerk had at last left them for other company. By midday it was very hot and they were feeling the full weight of their luggage. Not only were they walking as fast as possible but they had packed with Matton's promise in mind, that somewhere close by there would be a train to take them to a safe destination. Also, there had been a sharp night frost recently, and they had dressed with no certainty of the fine spell continuing.

All along the way there were little groups of empty houses, deserted by their owners who had joined the long trail of refugees. Presently Kurt stopped, too hot and tired to continue with his extra burden of a suitcase as well as the briefcase containing the papers and lists from Marneffe. He packed his coat and pullover in his rucksack and then went round to the back of one of the houses which was very quiet and evidently uninhabited. He found an unlocked door leading to a flight of stone steps into the cellar, and went down into the cool twilight beneath the house. Here, in a dark corner, he hid his suitcase under some boxes where it could not be seen.

When he emerged into the sunlight his friends looked at him a little enviously but declined to follow suit. Even Frau Meyerhardt, who carried her husband's treasured typewriter, continued to lug it along with the handle cutting into her manicured fingers while Kurt marvelled to himself at such a priority. An hour later she was regretting it bitterly. They were walking through wooded country now and Dr Halberstamm suggested that she hide it in the trees, anxious that they should hurry along to catch up with Matton, as they were still potential targets while daylight lasted. This time Herr Meyerhardt supported him, a little wistfully, Kurt fancied, and the typewriter was duly hidden in some thick bushes and the place memorised by various landmarks.

They walked on and on along a straight road with no sign of their erstwhile companions. Once, they heard more aircraft and in a sweat of fear dived simultaneously into a haystack for cover, but although there was gunfire there were no bombs this time. Kurt, hearing Dr Halberstamm's breath rasping with exertion, looked at him in alarm. The doctor told him quietly that it was his heart: he had had one coronary already, adding that that should be warning enough not to tumble in the hay like a youngster.

In the late afternoon they approached a T-junction and caught sight of some Belgian soldiers. Before they were close enough to ask which road they should take, the whole contingent began signalling frantically to them to keep clear. They had no option but to cut the corner and turn left, realising only as they did so why they had been warned off. The soldiers were in process of mining the road junction.

They hurried on, tired, hungry and tense with anxiety. Then, just as it was getting dark and they were wondering what to do for the night, they arrived at a fenced field full of people – at first glance Kurt estimated about two hundred of them; when he looked again he recognised Mandler and then several other familiar faces. They had met up with a large party from Marneffe.

Everyone was exhausted and frightened; no one had eaten all day and the children were crying pitifully. It was also growing cold now that the sun had gone down. But the herd instinct is strong, and even while Kurt and his friends questioned those in the field about what they were doing there, they were crawling through the fence to join them. No one knew where Matton and Verbist were; they themselves had been heard speaking German by some French soldiers who had taken them prisoner. This was not encouraging news: the field was cold and exposed – and not only to the weather. Kurt pointed out that if they stayed they were likely to be bombed at daylight by German aircraft when they saw an easy target. On the other hand, if they tried to leave they had been warned that they would be shot by the French soldiers.

Dr Halberstamm suggested that they went in search of the officer in charge. The question of who should do the talking was clearly one of whose French was adequate. Most eyes turned towards Kurt. A few dissenters who were by now so frightened that they were suspicious of everybody murmured that this was too great a risk: Pick had the all-important brief case (and possibly the money too) and might be tempted to escape by himself. They were in favour of sending Mandler with his forceful personality and boundless confidence. Interestingly, Mandler's inflated ego collapsed on the spot and he became reticent, even subservient, pleading his wife and child for excuse. Pick was the boss, he claimed for the first time; he had the better French and was good at handling people. Pick should go.

Kurt declared himself a volunteer, and immediately the Halberstamms and the Meyerhardts offered to accompany him. It was decided that there was safety of all sorts in numbers, and the five covered their escape from the field by crawling under the fence to mingle with the next large group of refugees walking down the road. They approached the guard cautiously, with Kurt as spokesman flanked by his four friends. The soldiers were sullen and inclined to adopt a threatening attitude, but in the end they agreed to allow Kurt alone to go to the farm where the commanding officer was spending the night. There was more difficulty here in persuading the soldier on duty to wake his superior, and even then Kurt had to coax this man to listen to him. Finally his desperation got through to the officer who took in, unwillingly, what was likely to happen in the morning. He glanced briefly at Matton's list of names and conceded grudgingly that his prisoners were indeed refugees.

Kurt stood firm until the order had been given to release them all, and when two soldiers had been dispatched to carry out this command, he walked out of the farm to join the other four on the road. There was no point in returning to the party in the field, and they decided to press on, walking automatically in the cold night air, almost in their sleep, for hour after hour in the dark.

The sound of lorries roused them to full consciousness and they approached quietly, keeping under cover. The noise came from two motorised columns of the French Army which had come along separate roads to meet where they joined at a fork. There was also the sound of voices raised in high dudgeon as the officers argued over which column should proceed in front of the other. Suddenly one of the soldiers sprang from his vehicle shouting a warning to take cover, which was instantly obeyed by everyone. Kurt and his companions waited just long enough to see the whole lot creep sheepishly back to their trucks a few minutes later. The sound that had alarmed them so much had not been German aircraft after all, but merely the throbbing of their own engines idling while they disputed the right of way.

Just before dawn they came upon several more heavy lorries standing in a row, empty apart from their French drivers who sat waiting in the cabs. Herr Meyerhardt looked at them longingly and wondered aloud whether they might ask for a lift. They were aching all over now, light-headed from lack of sleep. Kurt peered through the half light: the lorries were part of a convoy; he could see anti-aircraft guns and felt a strong reluctance to join a military target. He argued a little with Herr Meyerhardt but weakened when he looked at Dr Halberstamm and remembered his already over-taxed heart. Later he had ample reason to regret giving in so easily.

The driver of the last lorry told them they were on their way back to France and agreed to take them along, and as they clambered over the high sides above the wheels and helped the two women up behind the cab, even Kurt had to admit he was profoundly thankful for the rest. Their initiative was not lost on other little groups of refugees they were now passing every few hundred yards; from time to time the drivers stopped to take on board two or three more who had also been walking all night and could obviously go no further. Conversation was minimal with the jolting of the lorry, and they were all too tired to be concerned that they were the only German-speaking passengers, or that when Kurt spoke French to those who joined them his accent was noticeably foreign. Nor did it occur to any of them until it was too late that their very clothes, and Kurt's pale sweater and ski boots in particular, could mark them out as dangerously different.

In two or three hours they had been through Charleroi and it was fully daylight. They were being driven along a country road between open fields with little patches of woodland, in many of which nestled a smallholding quite hidden from the road and well camouflaged from the air as well. As they passed one of these woods on the left, with the gentle slope of a hill rising to the right, there was again the dreadful noise of aircraft ahead. The drivers all accelerated but the convoy had been spotted and already one of the planes was diving straight towards them. The lorries stopped and the drivers all jumped out and threw themselves into the ditch at the roadside. The terrified passengers, knowing full well what to expect, had no time to take cover, and could only cower into the sides of the lorries.

At the last moment the plane started to circle again in order to come in lower over them. As Kurt looked up his attention was distracted by a scuffle taking place beside him in the lorry, and he saw to his amazement that the Halberstamms appeared to be locked in mortal combat. For a moment he wondered whether one of them had snapped with the strain, until he caught snatches of their words coming in little gasps as each tried doggedly to roll on top of the other on the floor of the lorry. Both were frenziedly claiming the right to be a human sandbag rather than the one protected by it, each arguing that their beloved daughter had more need of her other parent.

Touched almost to tears at the sight of them, Kurt suddenly heard what sounded like machine-gun fire. Everyone looked up as the plane described a wide arc over the wooded area, and then realised that it was being attacked by anti-aircraft guns hidden among the trees. Instantly, the passengers sprang to the sides of the lorries and climbed over to take refuge in the ditch.

It was at this point that Kurt became acutely aware of the unsuitability of his clothes. He remembered that once before the pale raincoat had stood out as an easy target from the air. Quickly he stripped it off and flung it as far as possible from him before crouching in the ditch with his companions. There they waited, heads down, for the plane to manoeuvre itself into position again to strafe the convoy.

They waited. There was no sound at all, either of aircraft engines or gunfire, or of anything else to break the peace of the May morning.

Slowly it began to dawn upon them that the plane must have been hit, and had crashed out of sight on the other side of the hill.

CHAPTER 4

May-June 1940

The convoy continued steadily southwards, and by the time it approached the French border it was the morning of 14 May. Kurt and his four companions were standing immediately behind the cab of the last lorry, which they shared with about 15 others. There was no room to sink into a more restful position and they slumped wearily against one another for support.

Kurt, half dozing on his feet despite the jolting, noticed that they were coming into the outskirts of a small town, which he saw presently was Avesnes-sur-Helpe. He woke fully when the convoy stopped in a deserted alley, the engines were switched off and the soldiers jumped out. There was whispered speculation among the passengers about whether this was to be the end of the ride. Kurt glanced at Dr Halberstamm, wondering how many of their own little party were capable of walking any further.

The backs of the lorries were being let down and the order given to get out. The passengers, painfully cramped after the long night's journey, obeyed slowly for the most part, although a few of the younger ones clambered over the sides and came down via the wheels. Kurt, who would otherwise have been the last man off, joined these, arriving on the ground to find himself face to face with one of the soldiers.

The soldier had a gun and the gun was levelled at Kurt. He glanced round to find no-one else had been singled out in this way. The soldier signalled to him with the gun to get back onto the lorry, which was empty now except for his four companions. As Kurt obeyed he saw that they too were being held at gunpoint by the other soldier. The end of the lorry was replaced and the two soldiers got back into the cab. The engine started up and the five prisoners were driven on towards the town centre. Each read in the other scared faces, 'Why us? Where are we going?'

They whispered nervously among themselves without putting into words their own private fears. The two doctors were holding hands so tightly their fingers were white; both husbands tried to reassure their wives, giving no great impression of confidence themselves.

The lorry stopped in the centre of a square, along one side of which was the police station – a great barracks of a place, humming with activity. Evidently an incendiary bomb had fallen there not long before the convoy had reached Avesnes, for the police were still occupied with hoses putting out a small fire. The two soldiers got out of the cab; one stayed to keep guard while the other went over to talk to a policeman, returning with him to the occupants of the lorry.

It occurred to Kurt that there must be some trouble over their papers, in which case things could easily be set right. Although he had no passport, he had identity papers from Marneffe which he could show them. He started to explain that they were refugees; then he made a sudden move to open his briefcase. Instantly, the soldier whipped out his gun.

The effect was electric.

Suddenly the whole focus of attention was upon the lorry. Windows were flung open round the square and people leaned out. Bystanders drew back to a safe distance, pointing, while everyone started shouting and gesticulating excitedly. An innocent movement had provoked a major incident, with Kurt at the centre of it.

His companions turned to him in bewilderment, asking what was happening. Kurt replied that he did not know, but his imagination was leaping ahead. This was a border town, full of refugees. It would be buzzing with rumours of every kind, not least of German parachutists and Fifth Column activity. Everyone would be taut with fear and uncertainty – there had been an air attack upon them that very morning – and now there was this soldier pulling a gun on five strangers in their midst. Kurt realised ruefully that it must have looked as if he had made to draw a firearm himself. Moreover, he and his friends had been heard speaking German; worse still, he was wearing stout boots for walking – boots that looked suspiciously like those worn by paratroopers.

A consultation was in progress between the soldier and the policeman, snatches of which reached the five on the lorry. Kurt alone, straining his ears to hear the words, could understand what was said. Then, quite clearly, a whole sentence dropped into his consciousness:

'Nous les fusillerons toute-de-suite' ('We will shoot them at once').

Kurt's mind ceased to race. It was as if everything ceased; as if time itself had stopped. He watched the policeman who had spoken walk away. The five of them stood there waiting. The others had not understood; Kurt said nothing to them because there was nothing any of them could do.

He waited. No one will ever know, he thought. His parents would never hear that death had come to him on this sunny May morning in a truck in the middle of a French town. One moment he would be standing there, and the next – life would be snuffed out by the bullet's impact with his body.

The policeman was returning with five men who formed a row facing the prisoners. On the officer's command they took the revolvers from their holsters and loaded them. There was absolute silence in the square save for the click of the metal. On another sharp command the five revolvers pointed upwards. Kurt looked down at the little black hole in the barrel of the gun into which all the world seemed to have been concentrated. One thought occupied his mind: will it be instant oblivion, or will it hurt?

He felt a slight stirring beside him as his friends suddenly realised what was about to happen. In a voice of utter astonishment, Herr Meyerhardt said, 'They are going to shoot us!'

Kurt stared back at the round black eye of the gun. 'Yes.'

Beside him, Frau Halberstamm cried out sharply, 'No! They can't shoot us! We are Jewish refugees!' Her voice, uncomprehended and unheeded, rose to a scream of horror. They could not possibly do such a thing – they had a daughter who needed her parents.

The muzzle of the gun continued to gaze upwards at Kurt, fixing him like a snake about to strike. There was more screaming now, coming from around the arena, raucous shouts and even hysterical laughter. For the crowd too, all reality had been suspended: they roared encouragement to the policemen to shoot, gathering at the windows and in the street, chanting and screaming for the spectacle of a public execution.

Kurt waiting for death, saw only the little black tunnel from which it would come.

The policeman in charge prepared to give the order to fire. On the count of two there was a sudden silence, out of which a French Army officer appeared on the tarmac beside them.

'What are you doing here?' he demanded.

'We are shooting spies.' The five revolvers lowered their gaze to the ground.

'It is not for you to shoot spies. That is a matter for the army. I'll take over here.'

He walked briskly away, to the audible frustration of the crowd. The gladiators had not spilt blood after all. There were boos and howls of disappointed rage.

The five policemen opened up the end of the lorry, their faces flushed as if they had been drinking, their breathing heavy. Aroused to a frenzy of excitement, they too felt cheated of the climax to the incident. They jumped onto the lorry and

moved towards the prisoners, a frisson of renewed anticipation rippling round the spectators. This was not lost on the
policemen, who squared their shoulders and thrust out their
chests. They were the heroes now, they held the stage and
they would deliver the goods.

The biggest of them, a great thug of a man, advanced on
Kurt, homing in on the German Fifth Column spy in the paratrooper's boots. He grasped Kurt by the jaw with one hand
and began to beat him with the other, back and forth with
alternate fists, while from far away the crowd chanted, 'Kill
the Boche! Kill the German spy!' and roared again for
vengeance.

It seemed to Kurt that he observed these things at a little
distance from the scene. He saw the object that had once
been himself swaying from side to side with each blow, the
flesh swelling to a spongy purple until the skin broke, and the
policeman's fists ran crimson. He found himself counting
each smash to his face, detached from the event, conscious
only that the policeman must not have the satisfaction of
bringing him down. At the seventh blow, as his knees were
beginning to buckle, a squad of black troops arrived to take
the prisoners into custody. Kurt's four companions were
herded off the truck; he himself was dealt a final kick which
sent him sprawling on his hands and knees.

They were escorted, each with a guard, in single file to a
neighbouring building, and made to wait in a corridor, face to
the wall with their hands up. Each in turn was called into a
room at the end while the others were guarded by the soldiers with fixed bayonets. Kurt was kept till last, and as the
merciful numbness began to wear off, his arms ached unbear-
ably. Slowly he eased them lower, only to receive a sharp
reminder of the bayonet between his shoulder blades.

Such papers as they had were acceptable. Evidently the
details given by all five of them agreed. The soldier behind the
desk was satisfied that everything was in order.
Incredulously, Kurt enquired whether they might go.

The soldier seemed almost amused at the question. Surely
Kurt could see that that would not be in their best interest.

After all that had happened, if they were set free the mob would lynch them...

They were taken to a barrack-like building and put into a large upstairs room, empty except for two trestle tables behind which was a single chair. Kurt, still spitting blood and bits of broken teeth, was quickly helped to this, the two women comforting him as if he had been a little boy. Frau Meyerhardt knelt beside him, clasping his hand in hers, while Frau Halberstamm pressed his aching head against her motherly bosom.

Without any warning, their tenderness proved infinitely more devastating than the ordeal that had gone before, and Kurt suddenly found release in uncontrollable weeping. The easing, healing tears flowed unchecked through his fingers until, to his amazement, a salty puddle appeared on the bare boards at his feet.

For two days and nights the five of them remained at the end of this room, imprisoned by a couple of trestle tables with a guard at either end of the barrier. They were given no explanation for this treatment, nor were they given blankets, nor drinking water. When they asked for food they were told that the necessities of life were obtainable if they could pay. Kurt, who was clearly seen as the ringleader and attracted the most suspicion, had no money at all; the doctors had practically none, and Herr Meyerhardt just enough to provide an occasional meal to share among the five of them. Anyone needing to go to the lavatory was escorted to an unspeakable hole in the floor and was not allowed to shut the door. On the second day Kurt realised he was recovering when, figuring prominently in this scene, he was struck by the sheer absurdity of the two guards, one at each side of the open door, solemnly aiming their guns at an injured, unarmed man in a proverbially helpless pose with his trousers down.

The following day they were joined in their makeshift cell by another family who had also come from Marneffe. These were a very poor couple with their two children, uneducated

Kurt's grandfather, centre front, with some of his children and the staff of his bakery in Vienna, in a damaged photograph from the end of the 19th Century.

2. Kurt's mother, Friederike Hauser, with her brothers and sisters. Left to right: Franz, Oskar, Friederike (Frieda), Robert, Caroline, Paula.

3. Kurt's parents, Alfred and Frieda Pick, on their wedding day,
28 May 1911.

4. Kurt, at nearly two years old, 1 July 1914.

5. Château de Marneffe, 1939: the group who prepared the Centre for the refugees. Kurt is in the front row, fourth from the right.

6. M. Michel Matton, *Directeur* of Marneffe.

7. Château de Marneffe in 1985, now an open prison.

8. Château de Bassines, Méan, 1944, now no longer existing.

9. M. Eugéne Cougnet, *Directeur* of *L'Ecole Nouvelle des Ardennes* at Bassines

10. Entrance to Château de Bassines, with the bakery to the right of the archw

11. Kurt and Pamela on their wedding day,
11 September 1948.

12. Reunion at Marie-Thérèse's flat in Liège, 1985. Left to right: Marcelle Burette, Georgie van Liefferinge, Kurt, Pamela, Marie-Thérèse Tock-Malaise, the author.

13. Reunion, 1985. Left to right: Marcelle Burette, Georgie van Liefferinge and his wife, Marie-Thérèse Tock-Malaise, Kurt, Pamela.

and primitive at the best of times, and now exhausted and harassed beyond their capacity to be reasonable. To make matters worse, everything about the wife combined to raise the hackles of Herr Meyerhardt and excite his prejudice against them. She was grossly fat, loud-mouthed and vulgar, and Kurt watched with dismay as the dentist's fastidious nose wrinkled in disdain. The rest of the party tactfully kept the two couples apart for as long as possible, but inevitably the crunch came with the next mealtime. Herr Meyerhardt felt no responsibility for the new arrivals and simply bought bread and cheese for the five of them as usual.

There was a hideous scene. The couple wept and screamed that the Meyerhardts wanted their family to starve to death, and the wife had to be physically restrained from trying to scratch the dentist's eyes out. In the end Kurt managed to persuade Herr Meyerhardt to buy enough for everyone, but the damage done was irreparable, and the woman, ignorant and vindictive, swore she would never forget the insult of rejection to herself and her family. Later, when it was getting dark, they all lay down in a line on the hard, plain floor, too cold and aching and exhausted to worry any more about the company they kept.

The next night there was an air raid. Kurt heard the now familiar pulsing of enemy planes through the semi-conscious doze which was the nearest substitute for sleep the conditions would allow. At first he was not sure whether he was back on the lorry or in a ditch – or indeed whether this was reality at all, until the 'crump, crump' of bombs followed by a much louder explosion and the crash of breaking glass brought him hastily back to his senses.

He sat up with eight other silhouettes to see vivid flashes of gunfire through the now empty windows. The children woke bellowing with fright while their parents, far from soothing them, joined in the uproar, crying and cursing, until the noise indoors was almost as deafening as the attack. Kurt and the two doctors comforted the children and calmed the whole family as best they could, but there was no lying down again that night.

The air raid passed without further incident, but as the first grey light penetrated the cell, Kurt began to hear another sound which had been inaudible when there was glass in the windows. Clearly, there were people below them; how many he could not tell, but there was hysterical fear in their raised voices. He noticed too that their guards were in a different mood: they no longer sat watching the prisoners idly. They stood, hands jumping to their guns at any sudden movement within the cell, and when their colleagues strode in and out of the room they sprang to attention as if panic was in the very air they breathed.

Around midday a French tank driver was dragged in and thrown to the ground in an opposite corner. He already had a black eye and his nose was bleeding freely down his uniform. He was a deserter, Kurt gathered, and because they were unable to do otherwise, the prisoners witnessed two or three guards setting about him violently, and soon the other eye was tightly closed by the toe of a boot. The soldiers continued to kick and punch the now insensible body until the officer in charge saw fit to order them off like a pack of hounds from its quarry.

The next afternoon the same officer came back and roused the tank driver from his crimson patch on the floor. Sickened at the thought of what was to follow, Kurt was turning away when he realised that the unfortunate man was being helped to his feet. The officer then held out his hand which the other accepted. Kurt caught the words 'Mon camarade,' and presently they walked out of the building together, the one carefully supporting the other. Shortly afterwards there was the sound of a tank being started up, and through the open doorway they saw the two men drive away together. Theirs was not the only departure: throughout the evening there were more signs of the army withdrawing, and by nightfall there was silence.

At dawn the prisoners woke to find themselves alone.

To begin with they spoke in whispers, not daring to believe that their guards had really left them. Then gradually, as the light grew stronger, they became more optimistic, and after a little, as nobody came in, the couple with their two children got to their feet and simply walked out without a backward glance. The five friends discussed their chances in low voices; they listened, but there was nothing more threatening to be heard through the open window than a faint breeze.

'Well,' said Dr Halberstamm at last, 'what are we waiting for?'

They came out gingerly from behind the trestle tables, very stiff from the discomfort of their cramped quarters, like people who learn to walk again after a long illness. Beyond the door used by the guards they found a narrow staircase leading to a vault below their cell. Because the building was on a slope this was a cellar at one end and had a door to the outside world at the other. Here were the people Kurt had heard from upstairs; there were crowds of them taking shelter, the noise was frightening and the atmosphere daunting in the extreme. Kurt read the terror of war in every desperate face, explaining something of the soldiers' panic.

There was no doubt that the five had been noticed. Several men were pointing at them, and at Kurt in particular, gesticulating excitedly. He heard the word 'espions' (spies) frequently, evoking recent memories that caused his heart to lurch. They stood near the doorway, uncertain how to proceed, conferring in whispers. There were no soldiers present, only one armed guard in some sort of uniform, who was watching every move they made.

The crowd was growing uglier by the second. Much as he feared being shot for trying to escape, Kurt was even more afraid of the threatening gestures being made more and more obviously in his direction.

'Come on,' he said at last, 'let's get out.'

To be on the safe side he asked the guard whether they were free to leave, half expecting the man's hand to fly to his gun, but he merely shrugged and nodded. In a few minutes they were out on the road heading for St Quentin.

Their relief was short-lived. They had only been walking for a few minutes when they heard shooting and presently passed a soldier by the side of the road trying to staunch the blood from a leg wound. Round the next corner they found themselves in the centre of rapid crossfire, and turning, ran for cover. Kurt saw a café, and guessing that the door might be unlocked, raced into it. There were a few tables with bright checked cloths, and behind these a door which was slightly ajar. Kurt took two steps forward and then stopped. Through the opening came one of the biggest alsatians he had ever seen, its raised hackles lending it even greater size. Seeing a stranger, it lowered its head, the edge of its jowl lifting to reveal a set of extremely business-like teeth, from between which it emitted a low, threatening growl. Kurt needed no further discouragement: he leapt from the house, slamming the door behind him.

There was no alternative but to return to the vault. Coming in out of the sunshine it seemed darker than ever as they edged round the wall to find somewhere unobtrusive at the back. But as their eyes grew accustomed to the dim light, Kurt realised that they had been recognised by those nearest to the door. Snatches of sentences reached his ears, again containing the words 'espion' and 'camion' – the spy on the lorry was in there with them somewhere. By now it was no longer a murmur: it came from aggressive, hostile faces belonging to men with clenched fists and flexed muscles. They were trapped with the whole hysterical mob between themselves and the outside world. Angry voices demanded vengeance on the spy who had sold them down the river, the spy in the white pullover and the paratrooper's boots. Terrified, Kurt turned towards the wall, shrinking from the threats to hunt him down in the semi-darkness and savage him to a pulp that could never betray them or their country-men again.

Suddenly he had taken all that he could endure. His nerve snapped. Anything would be preferable to being beaten to death in this claustrophobic cellar. Grabbing Dr Halberstamm, he gabbled incoherently that he must die, and die instantly. They must have pills with them, he pleaded, cyanide or the like, that they could give him. Something that could kill, and kill quickly, before the mob lynched him.

The Halberstamms were stunned. Unable to understand the French spoken round them, they could barely grasp the danger Kurt was in, let alone that he was contemplating suicide. They told him helplessly that even had they wished to connive in such a thing, they could not do so. They were doctors; they had taken an oath; they carried no such tablets with them then or at any other time. The straight truth of this answer, negative though it was, worked like a cold shower on Kurt's reason. He began to gather up his shattered wits and to fight back. If he had been recognised by his clothes, then he must get rid of the offending garments. Swiftly, he pulled his feet out of the ski boots, kicking them away from him. The jersey, however, was another problem. To take it off would involve removing his coat first, all of which would attract too much attention. His only hope was to cut it down the front and push it back out of sight. He turned to the doctors again with another request, this time for a pair of scissors.

But the Halberstamms had seen plenty of slashed wrists in their time, and without hesitation they replied in one voice, 'No!'

It took Kurt fully ten seconds to persuade them of his intention to destroy his pullover rather than himself – ten seconds in which people were screaming, and crying mothers snatched their children to them; ten seconds in which a search was instigated and powerful torches were beamed up and down every man present, from his chest to his feet. Someone panicked near the back of the vault, shouting for a gun to shoot himself rather than surrender to the German spies. The cry was taken up all round: 'We don't want Germans here! German spies – out!'

In the darkness and confusion, Frau Halberstamm produced with trembling fingers a little pair of scissors, and Kurt butchered his white pullover, tucking the raw edges underneath his coat. The flashlights glared in his direction, hovered for a long moment, and moved on.

He sank back, his head resting against the rough brickwork of the walls. Far away, in another world, the vault gates were slammed shut and rumours sprang up that the German

Army was coming. In the solid safety of the vault he heard the noise of guns and all the storm of battle, listening unmoved while the Front swept overhead like a driving blizzard and passed away beyond them.

Afterwards, the silence was oppressive and charged with foreboding, like an icy grip on the nape of the neck. It told them nothing of what had happened up above, nor of what might lie ahead. They waited, reading defeat in each other's faces and transmitting wordless fears through eyes widened with terror. Some of the mothers, in a state of collapse, were crying soundlessly while their children whimpered and clung; otherwise there was the silence of interminable waiting for news they had no wish to hear.

When it came, it was in a form that no one had expected. There was a knock at the door – not a loud, authoritative demand to enter, but a timid request against the solid wood. At the same moment the door slowly opened, revealing a man standing on the threshold.

There was a gasp of fear from everyone who saw him. He was young and he was alone, but he was armed and the uniform he wore was German. After a brief look he went away again, leaving the door ajar. They went on waiting in the silence of uncertainty.

Presently the German soldier returned, and this time there were several others with him. One of these stepped forward, asking in the guttural broken French which was automatically threatening to the listeners: 'Are there any children in there?'

The silence disintegrated into the shrill screams of people who were by now half crazy with fear. The soldier held up his hand imperiously. They were not to alarm themselves, he said. The Germans meant them no harm; they had milk for the children. They were to come out, all of them, mothers and children first, and show their identity papers. 'Please,' he added politely.

So, thought Kurt, this was to be the end after all. Slowly, the vault began to empty, while he and his friends hung back, as if by delaying the moment of truth they might somehow seek to avoid it altogether. But there was not a doubt in any of their minds that this would be the end of the journey. They were Jews; they had no rights, no status, no defence and ultimately no option but to follow the rest outside. For them, this meant certain deportation.

At the door Herr Meyerhardt took over, and in his impeccable German explained to the soldier, man to man, that he had been an officer in the first war, these were his companions and they would like to know how to proceed. They were led to the sergeant who, having no instructions concerning Jews, ordered them to be taken to a prisoner-of-war compound. This turned out to be a big field on the outskirts of the town, surrounded by guards and full of French soldiers. Here the five of them sat down apart from the rest, and waited.

Unknown to the others, Kurt saw the final seal of their doom on his own person. Before the evacuation of Marneffe he had put in his pocket a few gold coins of his father's. Now, if they were searched, and never had this seemed more likely, he would certainly be accused of smuggling and thereby incriminate them all. He looked round. As he had expected, along the edge of the field a trench had been dug. Without a word he went over as if to use it for its intended purpose.

Presently one of the soldiers came and summoned them before the duty officer. Once again Herr Meyerhardt acted as spokesman, and a few minutes later the officer spoke to his subordinate. They had no instructions dealing with Jewish refugees, he said. Their orders were that civilians were to return to their homes.

There was no search. Kurt and his friends walked away free from the field with a trench in which somewhere there glistened unseen a little cache of hidden treasure.

In accordance with current German instructions to project an image of benevolent and correct behaviour, Kurt and his friends were led to a wholesale food store and invited to help themselves to whatever they fancied. They were very hungry; they were also deeply wary of such an offer. Without altogether passing up the opportunity of a much-needed meal, they took the minimum of simple food, fearful that a liberal helping of delicacies might lead them into the trap of an accusation of theft.

Having eaten, a great weariness overtook them and they walked to a nearby farm with the intention of begging beds for the night. It was a neatly kept little place, more prosperous than those they had become accustomed to seeing. The girl who opened the door to them, whom they judged to be the farmer's daughter, seemed frightened and bewildered; beyond her Kurt could see into the farm kitchen. There was the usual scrubbed tile floor and gleaming range, but what took his eye was the table, round which several men were sitting. This was spread with a feast such as the five companions had not seen in months: there was a ham, a loaf of home-baked bread and a huge pat of yellow farm butter. Those who were about to start this meal were all German soldiers.

Clearly, the farm was occupied, and these men had been billeted in it. Kurt quickly asked the way to the nearest town and the five of them left hurriedly. That night they slept in a barn with the straw pulled up round their ears for comfort.

Next morning saw the start of the long trek back. They had been directed to go home, and the experience of months had impressed upon them that if they acted with the permission of authority they stood a marginally better chance of staying free. Accordingly, they left Avesnes and headed for the only home available to them, namely Marneffe.

In the middle of the afternoon, when they had been walking for many hours, there was a commotion ahead of them and a German motorcyclist approached them, riding them into the ditch. In loud, text book French he warned all refugees to keep right back off the tarmac: the road was needed for the German Army. He was gone in a cloud of exhaust fumes, and Kurt was still translating the order into German for his companions when the heralded contingent arrived. The armoured cars, equipped with the most sophisticated weaponry of every kind, took on the aspect of a ceremonial procession, while the soldiers themselves, resplendent in their impeccable boots, held their blond Teutonic heads high, their faces as radiant as the round brass buttons on their uniforms.

Afterwards, the five companions struggled out of the gutter a little dirtier, their clothes a little shabbier than before, and walked on along the interminable road. As the last vehicle disappeared from view, Herr Meyerhardt announced suddenly that the German Army was without doubt the finest in the world. Nobody, he said, could hold a candle to them for efficiency and discipline. Kurt glanced at him curiously. Herr Meyerhardt was weary and dishevelled, his stout shoes worn through almost into holes. But, like the youthful specimens of his countrymen just passed, his handsome face was glowing with patriotic pride.

When evening came they met a party of nuns, and with Kurt as interpreter asked whether they knew of somewhere they might spend the night. The nuns directed them on to the nearest village, where they knocked at the door of one of the first houses. It was empty, although there were signs of recent occupation by the advancing army, for German newspapers had been left in one of the rooms. There was also enough food to provide a scanty meal with something left over for breakfast. The travellers refreshed themselves and retired thankfully. Upstairs were three bedrooms, and in a short time Kurt was sleeping like a baby in the luxury of a proper bed with a room to himself.

They walked out of the comfort of the house next morning into a world of utter desolation. The village had been deserted, the few elderly civilians who remained being so stunned with shock that they appeared barely human as they shuffled around, weeping tears of fear and anguish and despair for their ravaged homes and ruined lives. Cows, turned out by owners who had fled, wandered loose along the roads, lowing continuously with the increasing discomfort of their full udders. The day became hot; swarms of bloated flies crawled and buzzed; the stench of death grew sickening. German soldiers were clearing corpses from the streets, hardly able to drive away the starving cats and dogs that strayed among them. Kurt saw a bony mongrel keeping guard with savage loyalty over its dead master, and looked away as one of the soldiers settled matters with his revolver.

In every village the scene was the same, and the roads between were no better, rendered hideous by the bellowing of the cattle whose pain was now becoming intolerable, while those which had been abandoned in their stalls added hunger to the miseries of neglect. Late in the afternoon, when the travellers were themselves desperate for food, Kurt caught sight of a parcel on the ground. Thinking it might contain something to eat that had been dropped by other refugees, he picked it up eagerly and opened one end to investigate.

Inside he found a dead baby.

They spent the following night in a rented room at Charleroi, and slept a little, overtired and restless, missing the privacy of the previous night's lodging. At about 5.30 they were fully roused by the sound of planes, and literally drenched with sweat at the thought of another air attack, they got up and set off hastily, away from the town once more. There was no way of telling what was happening at the front, but even in the cold, grey light and desolation they could not bring themselves to believe that the British would be defeated. When the noise of the planes had gone their footsteps echoed in the streets so that the emptiness seemed brooding and unearthly.

They walked all day and towards evening reached the familiar Namur to Marneffe road, and presently caught up with a horse and cart driven by a farmer whom Kurt recognised. The two older men were completely exhausted: Herr Meyerhardt was in his sixties and Dr Halberstamm, though ten years younger, was feeling the strain on his heart at every step, and the rest of the party was in not much better shape.

Kurt greeted the farmer and asked whether they might take turns riding in the cart. The farmer demurred, his wretched horse being too undernourished to pull its present load with any ease. In the end he agreed on one condition: Kurt, as the strongest, had to go on ahead each time they neared a bridge and check that it had not been destroyed. This way, if he reported back that the road was impassable, they could go round by a different route, and the horse could be saved unnecessary toil.

Herr Meyerhardt took the first lift gratefully, bowing to the farmer's wife and politely asking permission to join her. He received no reply, the poor woman being quite oblivious of him or anything else. The shock of recent suffering had closed her mind against the horrors of the world and reduced her to something hardly better than a cabbage.

That night they lay in a barn, wide awake every minute with the dreadful noise of the now starving, anguished cattle. On the following day they passed the wood where the Meyerhardts had hidden their precious typewriter, but it was not to be found. Kurt's suitcase, on the other hand, was exactly as he had left it. He picked it up from the cellar and shortly afterwards they walked into Marneffe almost as if they had never been away.

In many ways it was as they had first known it. About a dozen of them occupied the same empty shell which still waited to be transformed, with the same lack of necessities for transforming it. There was no electricity; certainly the plumbing was as cussed as ever – and so too was M Bis who had remained there during their absence.

Over the next week or so Kurt talked to him, trying to discover what the best move would be. They talked round the issue carefully, like two dogs meeting, since Kurt was disinclined to ask his advice directly. M Bis, for that matter, was not naïve enough to give it, although he left Kurt in no doubt that he thought they should stay. Kurt aired the pros and cons of leaving and invariably the caretaker reinforced the case for remaining. Kurt weighed this opinion against the fact that M Bis (like the majority of his countrymen at that stage) was wanting to collaborate. In the end he was left with a vague unease about staying which he could not have explained except that he certainly did not wish to be beholden to M Bis.

He decided to walk to Huy and try to find out from the Germans what plans, if any, had been made concerning Marneffe. There he found that a complete takeover had been effected, with everything in submission to a German *Kommandantur* who had been put in as the representative of the Occupation Forces for the region. When Kurt informed him that the camp was now virtually empty, his reply was a shrug of the shoulders. He had no instructions, he said; Kurt could go where he wanted.

By the time Kurt returned to Marneffe, however, Fate had decreed otherwise. Compared with his recent travels, the walk to Huy and back had been nothing; nevertheless, it now proved to have been the last straw. The unrelenting forced march coupled with physical and mental strain suddenly combined to demand an immediate respite. Kurt retired to bed with an undignified and extremely painful complaint that prevented him from standing or walking any further, while sitting was entirely out of the question.

He remained immobilised for three days, being visited by everyone. There were no medical supplies, of course, but that did not inhibit his well-wishers from prescribing a bizarre variety of equally useless remedies. Even the two doctors were powerless: Frau Halberstamm clucked over him affectionately enough, but her husband, the patient thought, was positively heartless in his bracing assurance that he had yet to hear of a fatal case of Kurt's affliction.

Eventually the pain subsided somewhat of its own accord and he got up and went downstairs. There he found a girl who had been one of the wife-swapping set; he remembered seeing her walk out of Marneffe with somebody else's husband. At one time she had endeavoured to become very friendly with Kurt, offering to come and look after him if and when they all returned to Brussels. Kurt, whose sole interest in that direction had been centred on Mouchie, had coolly disillusioned her of the job's fringe benefits which she had clearly coveted. Now she was in a great state of agitation and treated him to floods of tears, begging him to help her as she was quite on her own with no one to whom she could turn. He listened sympathetically, for the evacuation had been traumatic for them all, and when she was calmer he accompanied her back to her room. Once inside, however, he began to discern that her desire for his company was not wholly because she was alone and afraid. He perched on one of the beds while she got into the other, and presently she was openly trying to persuade him to remain there for the night.

Suddenly Kurt felt very tired. It was dusk now and his knees had begun to shake with fatigue. He thought of the long walk back to his own room and of the many little flights of steps on the way to fall down in the dark. Worse still, he was being reminded more sharply every moment that although he was better he was not yet cured. Stretching out on her husband's bed he thanked her gravely for her hospitality, offering in return only the promise of disappointment. As darkness fell, she whispered to him that she was cold, begging him to join her. He capitulated, but not without honour. Reiterating his negative intentions, he did as he was bid, and was fast asleep before she could fathom the mysterious phenomenon of a young man with strictly monogamous inclinations.

In the middle of breakfast next morning, her husband suddenly walked in, having returned from Brussels to look for her. She confessed instantly to all that had never taken place the night before, and he instantly forgave her. She was absolutely delighted to have him back.

Kurt was almost as pleased to see him as his wife was. If unofficial transport was getting through from Brussels to Marneffe, then presumably the journey was possible in the opposite direction as well. His mind was finally made up: it was time to leave Marneffe.

The same breakfast brought a reunion for Kurt too. He was still chewing on the news the girl's husband had brought when a familiar figure approached him. It was the clerk who had been his ever-present shadow when they had evacuated the camp. The little man seemed unaccountably pleased to see him, and shook his hand with a manner that was almost ingratiating. He had, he confessed, an apology to make. It appeared that he had overheard a smattering of Matton's conversation with the two men from Brussels who had asked all those questions. Of course he had no notion of the incident at the Consulate. Putting two and two together he had come up with five, convincing himself that the villain of the piece was none other than Kurt. So suspicious had he become that he had taken to following Kurt around with the express intention of preventing him from doing any more damage. He had chosen the most certain way possible, and to prove the point he produced a gun from his pocket.

This he had had with him all along, he told Kurt, just watching for an opportunity to catch him red-handed. It had not been until Kurt had stayed with the rest when they had left Marneffe, instead of going away on his own, that he had realised his innocence.

'My friend,' he told Kurt, 'you are a very lucky man. You can have absolutely no idea how near you came to being shot as a spy'.

CHAPTER 5

June 1940-July 1942

A t the beginning of June, Kurt was once more living in an attic in Brussels. On his return there he had been lucky enough to run into Herr Winkler, who had also had a room in the select top corridor at Marneffe, and who was now living in a house in the rue Dupont. He told Kurt there was accommodation in the same house; Kurt made enquiries and moved in immediately.

It was a tiny room with sloping eaves that made it impossible to stand upright at one end, but the bed was large, there was a gas ring and a marble washstand with a supply of cold water from a little cloakroom half a floor below. There was even a stove he could light occasionally if he saved enough for the fuel, and the chimney coming up through the whole house gave a little steady warmth at all times. As in the rue Brogniez, the window was a mere skylight through which he could only see more roofs, the angle precluding a view of the street, but he had not taken the attic for its scenery, so this did not worry him. It was only later that he regretted the limited outlook, and that was for quite another reason.

The house was high and narrow, with two rooms on each floor. The other attic was empty when Kurt moved in; below him was an elderly aunt of Herr Winkler, and Herr Winkler himself had one of the rooms under that, opposite a policeman on the same storey. On the first floor lived Herr Winkler's old father and stepmother, and the owner of the house – a woman whose husband had left her – occupied the ground floor. A Russian locksmith in the basement completed the roll-call of inhabitants.

In many ways it was the same situation that he had left a year ago; he was still jobless and desperately poor, but on the plus side it was midsummer – indeed the attic was sometimes suffocating – and more particularly, he had friends. There was, however, a significant and sinister difference now. By virtue of the occupation, Belgium had become a projection of Germany, and in Germany Jews were counted as vermin. So his escape had been in vain; he had been running, as it were, on the spot. To all intents and purposes he was back in Germany, and to make matters worse, there was now nowhere else to run. He reflected despairingly that he might just as well have stayed in Vienna.

He continued, of course, to see a great deal of his four special companions, who thought him quite a hero, and the Winkler family were also friendly and hospitable, making a habit of inviting him in for coffee and a chat. The other two couples had settled in the district of Schaerbeck and were soon following their respective professions in that neighbourhood. The Meyerhardts had gone straight to the flat of some friends from Berlin, only to find that they had been sent to France for internment. The woman who held their keys told the Meyerhardts that although she could not let them into their friends' flat, there was another room to let in the same house. It was a nice part of Brussels and they took the room gladly.

The Halberstamms' first consideration was to be reunited with their adored daughter. After that they found a little furnished flat in a poorer part of the same area and worked in partnership among the local refugees.

Kurt himself had two immediate ambitions. The first was to reunite the erstwhile residents of Marneffe with the possessions they had had to abandon in the cellars of the château. He felt deeply responsible to Matton for this, having personally drawn up the necessary lists before the evacuation. His second ambition was to reunite himself with Mouchie. Understandably, he attended to the latter consideration first. He was becoming more and more concerned for her safety with all the alarming rumours that were being spread abroad about the fate of refugees, and especially since he had tried unsuccessfully to telephone her on numerous occasions. At last one day she answered his continual dialling in person; she and her family were safe and well - and she was clearly pleased to hear from him. Anxiety allayed, it was scarcely more than a formality to ask her what she had been doing since he had last seen her.

The casual tone of her voice left him unprepared for her reply. She had been arrested as an alien and had spent a short spell in prison, but her parents had procured her release, helped by the fact that her German father had gone to America. Everyone had thought that the Belgian line would hold, and that therefore the safest direction to take was north west. Mouchie's stepfather had managed to acquire a car with some petrol, and they had attempted to drive to France via Dunkirk. But the roads had been jammed with refugees and they had been in constant danger from German bombs, and had never got through. At Le Panne everything had come to a complete standstill and they had been overtaken by German troops. There had been a lot of bombing and many people had been killed.

Mouchie's family had turned round and come back to Brussels again.

Kurt went to the offices of the *Ministère de la Justice* and made enquiries about Matton. The clerk at the reception desk directed him to the Prisons Department where he learned that Matton had not yet returned. He was, however, greeted most cordially, particularly by one of the inspectors who had visited Marneffe and whom he had personally shown round. This man rejoiced in the good old Belgian name of Watson; he was evidently pleased to see Kurt again and listened with interest to his account of the luggage in the cellar. The upshot of this meeting was that Kurt was summoned to the same office a couple of days later. He arrived to find that M Watson had already hired a van to collect all the luggage from Marneffe and bring it to Brussels. Would Kurt like to go along to assist operations? Kurt agreed willingly, being known to Bis and familiar with everything at Marneffe. The only thing that puzzled him was the apparent scramble to get the job done so quickly.

A few days later Kurt went back to Marneffe and supervised the collection of all the residents' possessions. The men with him emphasised repeatedly that M Watson's orders had been that everything was to come. He had insisted that nothing of the camp was to remain, however trivial. Kurt pondered these instructions all the way back to Brussels. He became more intrigued when, in an astonishingly short time, Marneffe was in use again, this time as a prison. When Matton reappeared he was given the post of Governor there, and continued to keep in touch with Kurt for the rest of his life.

The more Kurt thought about the urgency with which all this was treated, the more he called to mind Bis's attempts to influence them to stay, and the rumours he remembered hearing about plans to change Marneffe. With the benefit of hindsight, a question formed in his mind: had Watson actually heard of plans to make Marneffe into a very different kind of camp from the one that he had known? He could not prove it, but the kindness he had received from the Department, coupled with the speed with which the proverbially sluggish wheels of civil service had turned, led him to believe that the inhabitants of Marneffe owed a profound debt of gratitude to Watson. If Kurt were right, he was responsible for deliberately making certain that there was no large vacant site for the Germans to use for their own ends.

Shortly afterwards, Marneffe Refugee Camp was wound up completely. In co-operation with the Prisons Department, Kurt was able to trace all the residents to reunite them with their possessions. When that was done nothing remained to give the Germans a clue that there had ever been 600 Jews at Marneffe.

Just as Kurt's life there was different this time, so Brussels itself had changed since the German occupation. The chaos of the month before was over, and gas, electricity and transport were all working normally again, but in a town emptied of men. Only those in selected jobs remained, most of the soldiers being prisoners of war, while the male Jewish refugees who were not already in camps had been interned in France, having enemy nationality.

The German mark was now legal tender as well as the Belgian franc. The Germans spent freely, especially on luxury goods such as silk stockings, quality clothing and furs. They also bought food, sending most of it home where there was little in the shops, although the country was enjoying temporary peace. With his empty promises that they would not be bombed, Goering had given his famous decree of 'guns before butter,' with the result that the occupying forces in Belgium were sending back food and everything they could lay their hands on to their hungry families.

At first the Belgian shops were well stocked with everything: it was, after all, a food-producing country and there was peace again behind the front. The Germans gave the impression of being good customers with plenty of money to spend. The small shopkeepers collaborated gladly, falling in with the new theory that the Germans had changed and were now friendly and benevolent. Business appeared to be booming – until stocks simply came to an end. Suddenly there was nothing more to be had; the sales turnover they had enjoyed became overnight a complete sell-out, and small businesses were left with nothing but what proved eventually to be a heap of worthless cash. The more astute (mainly in the large concerns) foresaw this happening and sold only against dollars. As these were only available on the black market because the Germans had called in all foreign currencies, their value soared.

Into this precarious situation Kurt arrived with nothing and no prospect of a job. Under the new regime he found himself entitled to unemployment benefit but this was pitifully inadequate and he yearned for something to do. Many young people found ways of supplementing what they received: there was a busy trade in the place Rogier, the rue Neuf and the place de la Monnaie for those who solicited German soldiers in the street and, acting as interpreter, took a commission for shepherding them to shops selling the luxuries they sought. Kurt rebelled against this practice from his innermost being. Not only was his instinct to have nothing to do with it but the thought of collaborating with the Germans in such a way appalled him.

There was also much soliciting of the more common sort – indeed the attic opposite Kurt's was soon taken by a mother and daughter. The girl had a *pied-à-terre* elsewhere, but there was very little secrecy about her profession. The authorities were well aware that all this was going on, and frequently called in those drawing unemployment benefit to do a day's work in return for their money. This took a variety of forms, some more acceptable than others. Kurt had nothing against a day in an office cancelling used ration stamps, but he detested having to hump coal for the city's old and poor, not only because of the time it took but because of the difficulty getting the filth off himself and his clothes. But there was one job that he positively enjoyed – alas, the least often demanded of him – and that was clearing hard-packed snow from the pavements. It was clean, healthy, outdoor exercise with the bonus of reawakening happy memories of home.

Having no stomach for the usual kinds of money-raising, nor even for the rewards of nightclubs and high life that those who indulged in such practices enjoyed, he endeavoured to find work that was regular and above board. The Jewish

Committee was now being organised under German initiative, and when Kurt applied there for a job he was given a written test. As far as he was concerned this turned out to be a farce, as the questions were all to do with Belgian culture and required a high standard of knowledge of Belgian history and geography, about which he knew practically nothing. Not unnaturally he failed miserably and was faced with the fact that he was accounted therefore totally unemployable.

Although he remained poor, he was now no longer destitute. His friends were good to him; he visited them often in the evenings and weekends, and their company not only sweetened life, but owing to their generosity largely sustained it. He played bridge, went swimming and enjoyed many meals at other people's expense, and because he disliked intensely the idea of being a kept man, he was meticulous in doing more than his share of washing up and any other little jobs that came within his scope. It all helped to salve his conscience, but he was still sensitive about the lean stripes in his curiously streaky existence, and nobody knew that if he bought a little present for anyone or even paid his way on a social occasion it involved missing meals altogether. He lived in dread of Herr Winkler – or even more painful to his ego, the Meyerhardts – passing by when he was coal heaving, although he had nothing worse to be ashamed of than an upbringing that was squeamishly respectable.

When suitably dressed, however, he was pleased to see the Winklers, and there was no doubt that they enjoyed his company. Kurt had never thought of himself as a ladies' man but he had always been a great favourite with older women, who were flattered to have a little attention from a young man with good manners. At Marneffe, Mme Matton had become quite kittenish whenever he had brought her back a few flowers from Liège; now there was no doubt that Frau Meyerhardt fancied him a bit. Even Frau Winkler flirted mildly with him in public and often persuaded him to go shopping with her on the pretext that he was an expert on clothing and could advise her what to buy.

His conversations with Herr Winkler also concerned financial transactions, but were of a less frivolous nature. Money was Herr Winkler's consuming interest and he confessed himself totally baffled by people who did not worship at the same shrine. He liked Kurt and respected his views while openly admitting that he could not understand him at all. Here was this well behaved, well spoken young man who had held down a responsible position at Marneffe, yet who now existed only on unemployment benefit and showed no interest whatsoever in earning anything to supplement his meagre income.

In spite of his penniless state, Kurt was suspicious of the whole concept of money making. As an end in itself he found it a senseless exercise, producing something of no intrinsic worth which had, moreover, a tendency to distort more important values. He knew that it was just Herr Winkler's attitude to money that could be used to fan the age-old flames of prejudice against the Jews. Having been brought up in a largely non-Jewish district of Vienna, Kurt had a foot in each camp, identifying with his Austrian compatriots as well as with the Jewish people, and had good friends among both. In this way he had learned that it is neither roots nor race – and certainly not wealth – that put a value on anyone, but rather the uniqueness of each human being. It was this respect for the individual that tied his hands now, preventing him from going into business with Herr Winkler. At a time when money would have meant a better chance of survival, not only enabling him to buy physical necessities but perhaps to ensure his very safety, he could no more have trodden people down in order to grab things for himself than he could have pushed to the front of the crowd getting out of Marneffe.

Bound up with this prohibitive attitude to cashing in at the expense of others was a strong sense of responsibility to prove that antisemitism was wrong. His own experience insisted that Jewishness was characterised not by hard business acumen but rather by a deep sensitivity and a caring for suffering humanity, without which so many artistic works and philanthropic concerns would have been lost to the

world. Looking back he could see how often this in-built
sense of service had landed him jobs of responsibility for
other people's welfare, and how often this could have threatened his own safety. Quite illogically, time and time again, it
turned out to be the very execution of this work which saved
his life.

But he was wary not only of money making but of the
Winklers themselves. When he had written to his parents
with the news that he was now living in the same house, his
father had replied with a note of warning. Herr Winkler's
father had once made a living in Vienna buying up the estates
of bankrupts at a knockdown price. Some of his deals had
been distinctly shady, ruthlessly exploiting helpless people at
this most vulnerable time in their lives.

So when Herr Winkler talked money Kurt listened with
caution as well as interest, discovering that the speaker was
open-handed to a fault while something might be gained
from it, but quick to wash those same hands if a deal misfired,
leaving others to foot the bill and answer for the consequences. Herr Winkler's generous tipping ensured that he
received VIP treatment wherever he went: the best table in
the restaurant, a changing cubicle at the swimming pool on a
crowded afternoon, a place at the head of any and every
queue.

Necessarily, a great deal of this privilege rubbed off on
Kurt, who was conscious of a debt of gratitude to Herr
Winkler for much hospitality he could never hope to return.
When Herr Winkler confided in him that he needed dollars to
pull off a highly profitable deal in silk stockings, Kurt saw an
opportunity to help two friends at once. Mouchie's stepfather was by profession a financial adviser and might easily
be able to get hold of the necessary dollars. He made tentative
enquiries when he next visited Mouchie; M Heckmann was
indeed extremely interested, having several clients who
needed Belgian francs badly and were very anxious to sell
their dollars at a good price. Kurt arranged a meeting
between the two men, quietly amused as he took his commission afterwards by Herr Winkler's satisfaction in handing

it over. Evidently he thought that Kurt was beginning at last to shape up as a respectable business man.

Next day Kurt was invited to visit Mouchie's family, which he accepted in high spirits, delighted that they should thank him with a lunch in his favourite company. When they sat down to the meal he noticed an envelope beside his place which he queried with his host. M Heckmann expressed surprise at such a question: Kurt had been the middle-man – the envelope contained his commission. Covered in confusion, Kurt hastily handed it back, explaining that he had already been rewarded by Herr Winkler. M Heckmann was speechless with astonishment. After that, Kurt arranged one or two similar meetings between the two gentlemen and received precisely nothing for his pains, both parties conveniently concluding that the other had paid him. Kurt's own conclusion was that he was not cut out to be a businessman.

Herr Winkler, however, persevered with his apprentice, taking Kurt round with him and trying to encourage him to sniff out promising deals. But Kurt was a disappointment to him, disliking intensely the competitive wheeling and dealing in which Herr Winkler revelled – if for no other reason because in the end it meant inevitably having to deal with the Germans. At last one day Herr Winkler took him out to lunch and dangled a bait of an altogether different size in front of him. He knew someone, he said, who wanted to sell a big holding of South American industrial shares. Would Kurt approach M Heckmann and find out whether any of his clients would be interested? It was a very big holding indeed, he coaxed as Kurt hesitated; there would be a lot of money in it for the middle man. Kurt raised his eyebrows a little and went on eating. 'About 50,000 francs or thereabouts,' Herr Winkler murmured.

Kurt laid down his fork, his interest aroused in spite of himself. He needed money desperately; apart from the necessities of life, money could tip the balance between survival and death. He asked for details of the owner of the shares. It was Herr Winkler's turn to hesitate. He assured Kurt that he could vouch for the man; he could not divulge his name but he knew him to be an honest dealer. Kurt insisted. No name, no deal, he said. Herr Winkler yielded and told him the name of the man concerned.

Kurt's mouth fell open. It was not a name he was likely to forget in a hurry. Herr Winkler's assuredly honest dealer was none other than the link man whose nose he had punched for cheating him over the jewellery. He refused point blank to have anything more to do with him. Herr Winkler was amazed at his attitude. What was the matter with Kurt, he wanted to know, adding, 'After all, money doesn't stink'.

But to Kurt some of it did, and there was an end to the matter.

He continued his close association with the family, but Herr Winkler made no further effort to involve him in business. Instead they discussed the development of the war and its effect on life in Brussels. Due to the all-pervading German propaganda hammered into them from every angle, they received an entirely one-sided account of hostilities. News bulletins were broadcast constantly in shops and other public places: a few bars of martial music would be interrupted by the now familiar 'Achtung! Achtung!' followed by an announcement telling of further impressive German advances on every front. Since it was forbidden to listen to the BBC – even to own a wireless was suspect – the general public was completely dependent for information upon these news items fed to it by the occupying power. Consequently, no one heard anything but German success stories blared out with unbelievable intensity, quite regardless of the truth.

Under the circumstances it was extraordinary that Kurt and his friends managed to retain their faith in an ultimate British victory, which at this stage of the war still seemed far from certain. They guessed that there must be a great deal being kept from them; also, they had an unshakeable belief in Churchill and the leaders of the British armed forces. All this combined to give them the hope they needed to survive, and even to live positively.

Yet while they hoped they also feared. Having no option, they listened to the unrelenting German propaganda, and at the same time strained their ears to hear what was being said between the lines, as it were, concerning anti-Jewish feeling. Occasionally some new official measure was imposed which affected them particularly, such as a curfew which was earlier for Jews. There were rumours of arrests and of Jews being drafted into forced labour. From time to time people disappeared. They began to realise that it was no idle whisper that the cellars of the Gestapo Headquarters in the avenue Louise were used for torture. If anyone was taken there, everyone was terrified.

Into this uneasy mixture of hope and dread there came back into Kurt's life his old friend Herr Spitz. Like most others he had fallen on harder times and had had to move out of the private hotel into a little flat of his own. This was just round the corner from the rue Molière, where Mouchie lived, and Kurt ran into him one day on his way to visit the Heckmann family. Herr Spitz seemed overjoyed to see him again: Kurt, he said, was the only person who didn't quarrel with him. Why did everyone he knew have to be so quarrelsome?

Kurt too was pleased to renew the acquaintance and began to visit him again regularly. Then one day as he approached Herr Spitz's front door he saw two people ahead of him on the other side of the road. He stood still and gazed after them as they walked arm-in-arm, laughing and chattering together. The young man was a stranger to him: tall, good looking and completely taken up with his companion. The girl was Mouchie.

After that he was forever seeing them, as if they timed their comings and goings by his visits to Herr Spitz. He was introduced to the boyfriend and not long afterwards learned that they were engaged to be married. He continued to see Mouchie from time to time, going around in a large group of friends, but it was no longer the same fun any more. There was a brief moment of satisfaction at a swimming pool when he took the opportunity of giving her a good ducking, but although it relieved his feelings temporarily, the situation remained unchanged. It did not even help to see that her fiancé stood by and watched him do it.

The worst part about it was that Mouchie's young man was everything that Kurt knew he could never be. He came from a rich Belgian family and was a promising medical student, a calling which Kurt himself might easily have followed had circumstances been different. His rival looked forward to all the openings for a prosperous, fulfilling life with Mouchie at his side. Not for him the low profile of the traditionally persecuted, the menial tasks of the penniless foreigner, the perpetual displacement of the refugee.

Kurt was no stranger to rejection and prejudice: he had been driven from his home, starved, frozen, threatened, insulted, imprisoned and beaten up, but the hurt of these things was as nothing compared to the pain of losing Mouchie.

It began to get cold again. The attic, no longer suffocating at night, took on a chill as the air condensed against the skylight and moisture trickled down the glass in continuous rivulets of silent tears. Kurt pressed his hands to the chimney breast, conjuring warmth, whether real or imagined, out of the brickwork. He was endlessly depressed by the damp of autumn, missing Vienna's crisp sunshine and the busy round of work at Marneffe that he had come to associate with Mouchie's presence.

His friends were at the same low ebb. The Halberstamms, for all the loving care they lavished on their patients, were constantly frustrated in their work by having no permits and no Belgian qualifications. This meant that they could only obtain the drugs they wished to prescribe through a Belgian doctor and frequently found themselves unable to provide the treatment they knew their patients needed.

The Meyerhardts had become resigned to the idea that they would not get out of Belgium while the war lasted. Like many others, they had put their furniture and possessions into a sealed container van in the international harbour in Antwerp until they could obtain their American visas. Now they decided they might just as well have the benefit of it, and they found an unfurnished flat in which to have their cherished belongings. With considerable difficulty they raised the fee for the two years storage and the removal date was arranged. Frau Meyerhardt told Kurt excitedly how much she was longing to have all her own things round her again, particularly her bedroom furniture which had been new when they had had to leave their home in Berlin. It was all painted in pale blue and had been wickedly expensive. She knew exactly how she would place each precious item...

But there had been a hiatus between the withdrawal of the Belgian Army and the arrival of the Germans, during which time utter lawlessness had prevailed. All the containers had been broken into and the contents damaged and looted. The seals on the Meyerhardts' van had been patched up well enough to deceive the customers into signing for acceptance of it, but when opened it was found to be quite empty. There was no insurance and no possibility of a claim against anybody. The Meyerhardts had lost everything they possessed. They had to move into a little rented furnished flat, and Frau Meyerhardt brooded for weeks over her pretty blue bedroom furniture, and cried and cried. Kurt comforted her to the best of his ability and the Meyerhardts warmed to him even more. Sometimes when he stayed late with them and was in danger of missing the curfew, he would spend the night on the divan in their sitting-room, waking to his own reflection in a mirrored wall intended to give an illusion of greater size to a very small space.

In contrast to their tiny home Kurt found their hospitality unfailingly generous. He slept better there than he did at home, thankful for the proximity of friends in undisturbed surroundings. Also, Frau Meyerhardt was an excellent cook and would send him off in the morning with the benefit of a good breakfast, making the most of such food as could be found. Herr Meyerhardt worked hard, even managing to scrape together some savings. After much deliberation he decided to use this money to acquire some gold coins, necessarily on the black market. Since all currencies other than

German and Belgian had been withdrawn, this was in itself a difficult and dangerous transaction. He buried them in the garden for fear of the Gestapo, whose raids on Jewish homes were becoming more and more frequent. Sadly, when the day came to dig them up they had all disappeared, causing Frau Meyerhardt many further tears.

Herr Winkler became one of Herr Meyerhardt's patients and introduced several friends to him, including one who insisted on putting all his savings into a denture made of platinum. Herr Meyerhardt obliged and when he finally fitted it the patient's jaw literally dropped. Because of the weight he seldom wore it, but even this was once too often, for one day he swallowed it. Alas, it was gone for good: he lacked the necessary perseverance to retrieve his costly investment.

The possibilities of platinum were not lost on Herr Winkler himself. He had a bunch of keys made of the stuff which could scarcely be lifted from his desk. In his case, of course, it could hardly be said to have represented his total assets – indeed Kurt never ceased to be amazed at his opulence. When his old father died, Herr Winkler moved out of the rue Dupont into a pleasant modern flat and enlisted Kurt's help in choosing the most elegant antiques for every room, including a complete set of genuine Chippendale chairs. It was sheer delight to Kurt to see and handle lovely things again, and meant far more to him than being taken by Herr Winkler to all the best black market restaurants, where there was real cream in the cakes and real coffee to wash them down. Wherever they went Herr Winkler would grease liberally every outstretched palm, murmuring as he did so that no engine runs without oil. As a result he was received with pleasure in the best circles, for although he did business with all the German top brass – as Kurt knew perfectly well – it was never Winkler himself who carried out the deals. He had a go-between, an unsuspecting little Belgian clerk, who soon acquired such an inflated idea of his own cleverness in getting a share of the big money that his eyes were blinded to things he should have seen.

The rest of Kurt's friends struggled like he did to make ends meet. By the end of 1940 so much food was disappearing over the border into Germany that everyone in Belgium was not only hard up but becoming decidedly hungry. Slowly, the image that the Germans were trying to project was beginning to wear thin; memories were revived of German atrocities during the First World War and it was now thought definitely unpatriotic to go to work in Germany. Bit by bit anti-German feeling developed. Overnight, slogans appeared on walls, V-signs were painted on pavements. The Germans insisted that this victory was theirs, so the perpetrators added an A to denote victory to the Allies. But the Germans pretended now that this stood for 'Victoire Allemande,' although their stock of goodwill had run out and opinion had finally hardened against their regime. In spite of the bombardment of propaganda, too many tales of horror were filtering through to be ignored. The tide had turned against the occupying Germans and Belgian resistance began to gather strength.

Kurt and the Meyerhardts met often to play bridge. It took their minds off the continuous, harassing fear of their uncertain future, and provided a forum for the exchange of information on new developments and rumours concerning refugees. Prior knowledge of such regulations could mean the chance to take avoiding action in time. Several people who came on these occasions had useful contacts, including a couple called Sternberg whom Kurt liked particularly. They had a little boy and were great friends of the Meyerhardts, and as Dr Sternberg held a high position at the Jewish Committee, he was an invaluable listening post in that quarter.

One night at the end of the rubber, the Sternbergs stood up to leave and suddenly announced that it had been their last bridge evening. In the shocked silence that followed, Dr Sternberg told them that he had got hold of a reliable plan to escape into Switzerland. When pressed for more information he would only promise to send details when they had arrived safely.

Later that night Kurt and the Meyerhardts discussed what they had heard in hushed voices, stunned by the implications of what Dr Sternberg had said. Either it was a very safe scheme indeed, which might therefore be of use to others when it had been proved, or else there was a frightening alternative. As Dr Sternberg was in contact with the German authorities through his work, he might have knowledge of some sinister plan. An escape of this sort was at best extremely dangerous – one could never be sure the whole thing was not a trap arranged by the Germans. On the other hand there were people ready to concoct a fake escape route for their own gain. Dr Sternberg would hardly have been likely to take such a risk with the lives of his wife and child unless the future for them all looked terrifyingly black. Kurt and his friends stared round the room at each other, the unspoken question hanging in the air between them: what was it that Dr Sternberg knew?

After ten days of anxious waiting there was still no news, and their hopes of hearing any more from the Sternbergs grew cold. There would have been no difficulty about sending a coded letter from a neutral country. Whatever had happened to them, they left an ache among those who had known and liked them, and at the same time the hideous question remained unanswered: what could be going to happen that was bad enough to justify Dr Sternberg taking such a risk?

Towards the end of 1941 the Jews in Brussels were becoming increasingly aware of a build up of pressure against them. More arrests were being made on smaller pretexts and there was a general tightening of anti-Jewish action. Those who earned commissions soliciting German soldiers on leave and introducing them to the big shops ran an even higher risk of being arrested on the spot, while even Jews walking about minding their own business were liable to be picked up for no particular reason. It was dangerous to gather in groups where Jews were likely to be found meeting, for fear of being rounded up *en masse*; more terrifying still was the Germans'

new practice of cutting off a couple of streets at a time and snatching every Jew caught in the net.

All this time Kurt had kept in touch with M Watson, going to see him occasionally at the *Ministère de la Justice* to discuss the latest developments of the war and to discover in advance, if possible, any new anti-Jewish moves being planned. Watson was in close contact with the underground movement in Brussels; he trusted Kurt and passed on to him much information that was helpful, including copies of the underground's newsletter. This Kurt would conceal in the heel of his shoe in case his pockets were searched on the way home, and later share with his friends. It was printed on paper thin enough to be flushed easily down the lavatory at the end of the day, but it was nevertheless dangerous material to walk around with, however well hidden. Indeed Kurt was disinclined to walk the streets at all because of the risk of quite arbitrary arrest. When he told Watson this, the other nodded agreement and dropped into the conversation that in a few months the Germans would start deporting Jews to the east. He said it so casually that Kurt did not register that this was a vital warning until it had already started to happen.

All the same, when he heard about a vacancy in a small business run by a Jewish family in a workshop behind their house, he applied and was deeply thankful that his reputation for reliability secured him the job. The firm employed three or four men and produced tiled splashbacks in metal frames to go behind cooking stoves. Kurt's relief lay not so much in having something to do, wonderful though this was, but in the safety of having work at all. While he was not earning there was always a danger that the Germans would demand a list of those who were receiving unemployment benefit and draft those on it into labour camps, especially if they were Jews. Also, he was now no longer a walking invitation to any German on a cleaning-up mission. Better still, the other workers were not Jewish and the workshop was in a non-Jewish quarter of Brussels; it was most unlikely that the Germans would come looking for Jews there. As he travelled to and from work in his shabby secondhand salopettes he was indistinguishable from the ordinary Belgian working man.

Occasionally, as he changed out of his overalls for an evening with friends, the unworthy thought crossed his mind that Frau Meyerhardt might not have greeted him quite so enthusiastically had she met him in the street an hour earlier. She might have been even more shocked had she discovered that he now indulged in the unbelievable luxury of going with his mates from work to sluice away the week's grime in a tub of hot water at the public baths.

A boy of eighteen taught him his job. He had to assemble the splashbacks by inserting the tiles into chromium frames screwing them together with the help of a pair of pliers. The metal came in sheets which were cut into strips; some of these were bent into frames and soldered at the corners by an old man. Some were used to make washers, and part of Kurt's job was to work the machine which first punched a hole in the metal and then stamped out the washer round it. To begin with he was awkward and the metal strips were sharp and wayward. He cut his fingers trying to advance or retard the metal as it travelled through the machine, in order to line up the washers with their respective holes. When he timed it wrong the hole came too near the edge and the machine stamped out useless little discs of its own design. After a few weeks he had the hang of it and was competing in speed with the boy who had taught him.

When lorries arrived with supplies he would help unload the materials and bring them inside. The sheets of metal were so cumbersome and heavy that the only practical way to carry them was on his head. Experience soon taught him that eight at a time was the limit: the pressure of more than that made his nose bleed, and besides if they became unbalanced the raw edges sliced into his hands. So he learned quickly, thankful not only for employment and wages but for the camouflage the job provided. The owner's mother adopted him immediately, paying him by the hour to scrub the stairs after work, using a scouring powder which was made on the premises from finely-ground broken tiles and sold as a by-product. She also rewarded him with hot soup from the family kitchen, deliciously welcome at the end of a long shift.

Although he now spent most of the day at work, whenever he was in his attic he risked being trapped by a Gestapo raid. Once he heard the doorbell ringing loudly downstairs and leaped to the skylight in a panic to see who was in the street below, only to find that the angle of the roof cut off his line of vision. For a wild moment he considered climbing out and hiding among the chimney pots until the danger had passed, but examination showed this to be totally impractical, the slope of the roof being even more hazardous than staying where he was.

Presently he tiptoed to the door and opened it a crack to listen. To his further horror someone was asking for him by name. He hovered helplessly between the door and the skylight for an interminable age, and then his landlady called upstairs to him and he could tell by the relief in her voice that she was on her own. While his breathing gradually subsided she told him it had been a foreign gentleman, who was passing through Brussels. He was the friend of a friend and had enquired whether Kurt would care to meet him a little later at the Gare du Nord where he would be in the station restaurant.

By now pleasantly intrigued, Kurt did as he was invited, and found waiting to see him a friend of the old family friend Herr Weninger, *Generaldirektor* of the bank in Vienna, who had warned his family in the nick of time to withdraw their money. They shook hands and Kurt asked eagerly for news of home. The other came straight to the point: the news, he told Kurt quietly, was about as bad as it could be. Herr Weninger had a message for him: Kurt should do his best to get out, and to get out fast. He urged him to try to get to Switzerland as soon as possible. Then he handed him an envelope from Herr Weninger and was gone almost before Kurt had had time to thank him.

Back in his attic Kurt opened the envelope to find a wad of bank notes. The memory of the Sternbergs was still vivid in his mind, otherwise he might have been tempted to take Herr

Weninger's advice. As it was he knew such an idea was quite out of the question. But he was badly in arrears with his rent, and although his landlady was always understanding about his situation, it went against the grain to be in debt. He went downstairs and gave her the whole lot, and slept that night with a lighter heart than he had known for months.

A few days later Brussels came out in a rash of posters decreeing that from the beginning of June all Jews must wear yellow stars which had to be clearly visible at all times. There was no likelihood of infringement of such a regulation: occupied Belgium was a police state in which everyone was obliged to show papers whenever the authorities might ask to see them. Everyone was in permanent danger of being stopped and questioned. If a Jew's identity card showed that he should be wearing a star, then he could expect the very worst to be in store for him.

On Sundays Kurt and the Winklers often took a walk along the avenue Tervueren, a pleasant, tree-lined road leading to a park. They saw no reason why the yellow cloth badges, sewn securely to their lapels, should alter this practice, and on the first Sunday in June they were strolling between rhododendrons in full flower when they began to notice the unwanted attention they were attracting. Little groups of German officers passing by stopped talking and stared at them, making audible comments on the lines of 'What do those Jews think they are doing here?' This was upsetting enough, but far worse were the looks they were getting, which spoke more eloquently than any words could express. Kurt had never before seen such hatred and disgust in human faces. They might have been looking at a sewer full of rats.

It was the shortest walk they had ever taken, and their last in the avenue Tervueren. Without another word they bolted in the opposite direction. Frau Winkler tripped on a kerb-stone and Kurt, steadying her, saw that her eyes were blinded by tears of fear and hurt. Rather than face any more walking in public, they squeezed onto a tram already full of Belgian passengers, and tried to stand unobtrusively together. But the yellow stars with the black 'J' in the centre were too blatant to pass unnoticed, and as the tram started there was a sudden surge of movement. Kurt, daring to glance up, caught his breath. More than half the passengers had risen to their feet and were enthusiastically offering their seats to the Jews.

He lay awake a long time that night, haunted by the staring faces and by the implications of the yellow stars. Also, strangely, there was the recurring picture in his mind of a man he had not seen for many months. The shock of expulsion from the avenue Tervueren had brought back memories of the evacuation of Marneffe with its similar fear and uncertainty. For some reason his uppermost thought was of Obler, the ruffian who had worked in the camp laundry. Kurt, in obedience to Matton's instruction to bring up the rear, had had ample opportunity to observe the general exodus. Not surprisingly, those at the front had been mainly the childless, the young couples, and especially the physically fit. He remembered Obler being among the very first to leave. He had set off at a smart pace, the muscles in his legs and back strengthened by his work at the camp to maintain his position effortlessly ahead of the rest.

Kurt, of course, had not seen him again, but recently he had heard further news of him. Obler and a small group had remained well ahead and had walked into France where they had been interned. The camp had been so appalling that many of its inmates had risked their lives trying to escape. Obler, with his brute strength and ruthless egotism, had been one of those to succeed, and had come back to Belgium. Here he had been arrested for returning without permission and had been sent to the concentration camp at Breendonk.

Kurt tossed sleeplessly on his attic bed, unable to rid himself of the image of Obler's great greasy hulk snarling at everyone who crossed him. Obler did not look Jewish with his blond hair and tough Saxon build. When he scowled and threatened, Kurt thought, he had looked as menacing as the Germans had that morning, his face like theirs disfigured by hatred and outrage. Much as he had disliked Obler, the questions nagged Kurt's mind: how does anyone behave under stress, his life continuously in the balance? Who may judge the moral standards of a man pushed to the furthest limits of his sanity?

Years later, after the war, he heard the rest of Obler's story, lending a new poignancy to his restless questioning that night. With his physique, coupled with a brutal insensitivity, Obler had contrived to become a *kapo*, or foreman, in the concentration camp. This had given him the apparent advantage of power with privileges, but in reality it turned out to be a truly ghastly position. He walked a knife-edge of responsibility, collaborating perforce with both sides at once: if he were too harsh he was in danger from his colleagues, if he were too lenient he risked losing his position and being punished horribly by the Germans. It had been too much for him. He simply could not cope with the pressure of such moral dilemmas. He misused his authority and became a sadistic bully. When the war was over he was tried by the Allies and hanged.

How much was the fault of the man, how much of circumstances? And how much better, Kurt wondered again and again, would he himself have done, with Obler's disadvantages rather than his own charmed life?

With the advent of the yellow star came more stringent restrictions for the Jews. From now on they were only allowed to live in certain towns, while those outside had to declare their whereabouts to the authorities and obtain permission to remain there. The resulting concentration of Jews in particular areas meant that arrests were easier to make. There was no safety in keeping with the herd – it was positively dangerous, being as it were already rounded up. Kurt and his friends whispered endlessly about the possibilities of getting out and discussed, panic-stricken, how they might acquire false papers. Overnight Kurt's job had ceased to be the godsend it had appeared: marked by the yellow star, he was now in danger every time he travelled to and from work. He remembered suddenly what M Watson had told him about the imminent deportations and realised that it had been no idle small-talk.

In the end it was Herr Winkler with his wealth of contacts who provided the first clue to a solution. He told Kurt one evening that he had heard of a job going as baker in a boarding school in the wooded countryside of the Condroz. Kurt, his hopes rising sky-high, stifled any feelings of inadequacy he might have felt and left Herr Winkler in no doubt that he would like the job.

In a few days he received a message summoning him to the Jewish Committee for an interview. Here he was seen by the headmaster, M Cougnet, a soft-spoken man with a gentle, bearded face. It was a long interview, during which Kurt saw fit to tell him at one point that his only possible claim to suit-ability for the job was that his grandfather had been a master baker. Otherwise they discussed what seemed to Kurt to be totally irrelevant matters, although all the time the mild blue eyes searched the applicant more thoroughly than any ques-tions. At the end M Cougnet sat back, apparently satisfied. He told Kurt frankly that so far he liked him best, but that as several others had applied he had to see them first before he made a decision. Would Kurt like the job?

Once again there was no hesitation in Kurt's answer. M Cougnet promised to write to him as soon as possible, reminding him as he left that if he were successful he would need a German permit to live and work at Bassines.

Two days later the first deportation orders started to arrive. They were individually addressed to selected people apparently at random, ordering them to be available for work in Germany on a particular date, with the threat of a concentration camp for those who did not comply with this instruction. One of these orders arrived for Herr Winkler's niece, a child of about fifteen. She was to report on a certain day at the assembly camp at Malines. The house in the rue Dupont was thrown into confusion as the family rallied round, intent upon obeying everything to the letter for the sake of the girl, and indeed for the safety of them all. Frau Winkler provided some strong shoes that would fit her, someone else had a rucksack she could take. Kurt had met the girl: she was shy and rather dull, and his heart went out to her, the more so because he thought the hope of a job might exempt himself from similar selection. Some time later they discovered that all those who reported were sent straight to concentration camps. Herr Winkler's niece was never heard of again.

When the assembly date came, Kurt realised that not everyone who received orders would report. The result, he knew, would certainly be that the Germans would make up the numbers with on-the-spot arrests. He still had not heard from M Cougnet, and he dared not go out in the street wearing his yellow star. Nor did he dare to sleep at the rue Dupont any longer for fear of being trapped in the attic if that district were chosen to make the mass arrests.

Strangely, it was hope rather than dread which took on a new meaning for him now. He had to get out of Brussels, therefore he had to believe he would get the job at Bassines. Everything depended on a favourable letter from M Cougnet, and in the meantime he had to act in confident expectation of success – without being caught.

He decided that it was time to go underground. The Belgian lad with whom he worked did not seem surprised when Kurt asked if he would give him his identity card. Kurt had noticed that it was old and tatty so that the photograph could have been of practically any boy of that age. The boy agreed to consult his mother that evening, and the next morning he handed it over. Kurt knew that he would have to report the loss of his card to the Belgian police, and he gave him strict instructions that if necessary he must say that the Jew he worked with had stolen it, rather than bring trouble on himself and his family. Even so, it would take courage as well as kindness to carry off the deception; Kurt gave the boy his father's gold pencil and asked him to accept it as a memento. Then he tucked his yellow star out of sight and made his way to the house where Herr Spitz lived.

Herr Spitz's landlady was all smiles when the nice young man who was a friend of the old gentleman called. She was very sympathetic when he told her that he had the decorators in at home and simply had to get away from the smell of paint for a few days. She showed Kurt to a most elegant room, comfortably furnished and with hot and cold running water. He looked at his star-free reflection in the long mirror in this luxurious apartment, and he fingered the Belgian identity card in his pocket. Then he went out again and spent the rest of the day and a great deal more money than he could afford in a delightfully plushy cinema where no German would ever have dreamed of going to look for a Jew.

On each of the next two days he returned to the rue Dupont to enquire whether there was any mail for him, but there was no word from M Cougnet. The following morning he ran into Herr Winkler who told him he had heard through the Jewish Committee that the Germans had clamped down on work permits altogether.

There was still no letter for him. He went slowly back to Herr Spitz's house and willed M Cougnet to accept him. He had no alternative future and behind him his boats were now burnt. He had to get out of Brussels and he had to have somewhere else to go. He tried to put Herr Winkler's latest information out of his mind.

By the next day his optimism had begun to crack. He went to the rue Dupont more from force of habit than because he expected a letter. He felt sure that M Cougnet must have given the job to someone else by now, and in any case he could no longer obtain a permit. Also, he had to face the plain fact that he was not a baker.

He arrived to find his landlady in tears, too upset to tell him what was the matter. When he had coaxed her into drying her eyes he discovered that the cause was none other than himself: it seemed there was a registered letter for him and she was convinced that his deportation papers had arrived. Kurt almost snatched the letter from her. It had been in the post for a couple of days; he was to apply for a work permit at once as he had been accepted at Bassines. His landlady wept again with joy when he told her the letter was good news and no one was going to be deported. In high spirits, she suddenly embraced him and as they both laughed with relief she remembered that there had been a postcard for him as well.

He read it, and then read it again, his mind rejecting the sense of the words he saw. The card was from an uncle and came from Theresienstadt in Czechoslovakia, telling Kurt that his parents had been deported and were there too. Theresienstadt had the reputation of being a 'good' concentration camp – it was a kind of show-place used by the Germans to boast of their decent intentions. Nevertheless, it was still a concentration camp, and later he found out that almost certainly it was merely a platform to Auschwitz.

For security reasons Kurt destroyed the postcard. He tore it into a hundred tiny shreds and flushed it down the lavatory with the same sense of revulsion as if it had been a poison pen letter.

He made up his mind that he would go to Bassines, come what may. It would have to be without a permit and without a single soul, even his closest friends, knowing where he had gone. If all else failed he would offer his services as a farm labourer when he got out of the city. He went out and bought a rucksack with the widest straps he could find.

Now that the decision was made, hope returned. He had one last leap to make beyond the point of no return. For some time now he had kept his parents' valuables hidden in his room against a financial emergency. It would be far too dangerous to take them to Bassines; he had to decide with whom he could safely leave them. So far, he had stayed strictly on the right side of all the regulations; from now on he was uncomfortably aware that things would be different. He had someone else's identity card and was proposing to go and live where he was not allowed, and without a work permit. In all probability he would never come back. It was really a question of to whom he should leave all that he had in the world. He made up his mind he would give everything to Mouchie, and then he went round and asked her to keep the things for him while he was away for a little.

On the morning of 28 July he walked to the station and bought a ticket to Les Avins-en-Condroz. It was his thirtieth birthday.

The train was packed. He stood in the corridor, carefully turned away from his fellow passengers, his star only partially visible under the wide strap of his rucksack. At Namur they came to a halt and there was a long delay. It was very hot and Kurt longed to take off the rucksack, but dared not remove it and reveal his yellow star. The station was humming with Germans walking up and down on duty, their eyes raking the crowds on the platforms and gazing in at the train windows as they passed. Kurt wriggled back a little deeper out of sight and tried not to look down to check how much of the star was showing. He watched the soldiers out of the corner of his eye and longed for the train to move away.

There was a sudden jolt; in an unguarded moment Kurt looked up eagerly – straight into the eyes of a passing German soldier. The man had surely seen the relief in his face, if not the yellow star, for he stopped abruptly, looked Kurt up and down and treated him to the kind of insolent stare which was becoming all too familiar to him. Kurt, his mouth dry, gazed determinedly over the man's shoulder, silently begging the train to move again. He saw the soldier raise his arm and point towards him, while the platform began very slowly to slide a little to the left. The German was now exactly opposite the carriage door; he took a brisk step towards it – and then at last the train was gathering speed. It had already left the station by the time Kurt felt his next heartbeat drumming in his ears.

He had had enough. At Ciney, where he had to change onto the branch line to Huy, he went straight to the station lavatory and ripped the yellow cloth star from his coat, carefully picking out the tell-tale threads that remained. While he waited to make sure of the complete disposal of the star together with his incriminating identity papers, it occurred to

him that it was becoming a grim habit to consign his unwanted
property to the nearest Belgian plumbing.

He was no longer a Jew. The young man who stepped off the
train at Havelange possessed a totally new identity.

The ticket collector told him that the Château of Bassines
was several kilometres away in a little wood. It was very hot
and dusty; worse, the road lay between open fields without a
scrap of cover anywhere. The place was lonely and remote,
but to a Jew who had destroyed his star and had another
man's identity card, it seemed certain that there would be
Germans waiting to spring at every turn. He acknowledged
that it was an unreasonable fear, but he was utterly vulnerable
to it as he walked with the trepidation of someone on a dark
night, prey to the primitive instinct that fears the presence
of the unseen hunter lurking everywhere. It was with
mixed feelings, therefore, that he reached the shade of the
trees and realised he must be nearly there. There were
no signposts to indicate his whereabouts, nor anything to
show that there was a building among the trees at all, so
that he came suddenly upon the school, with no prior
warning that he had reached his destination. The moment
of truth had arrived. He had to face up to the distinct possibility that, far from welcoming him, they might easily throw
him out again for having come without the necessary German
permit.

The château was built on a grand scale and must once have
been a fine property. Kurt walked through an archway under
a clock-tower and found himself in a stable yard where some
small boys in shorts and muddy shoes were kicking a football
around. They stopped when they saw Kurt, and a tall lad who
was much older than the rest came over to him. He told Kurt
he was M Cougnet's son and went to fetch his father.

When M Cougnet arrived in the yard he shook hands with
Kurt, evidently pleased to see him. Kurt confessed that he
had come with false papers, having had to destroy his own.

M Cougnet shrugged, as if to say that identity papers were of very little moment to him. Kurt took a deep breath and continued doggedly that he had no work permit, explaining that since the deportation orders, no more had been issued.

M Cougnet looked at him quizzically. Had Kurt received a summons? he asked.

'No,' Kurt replied.

If he had, would he have gone?

'No.'

The headmaster smiled suddenly, a peculiarly charming smile.

'Then stay,' he said.

PART III

Bassines and Liège

CHAPTER 6

July 1942-October 1943

Making bread had two things in common with making splashbacks, Kurt found: both were extremely hard work and the success of each depended upon precise timing. Twice he watched M Cougnet's eldest son, Pierre, demonstrating the process, and the third time he worked by himself under supervision. After that he was on his own, for Pierre was a teacher in the school and Kurt had been hired to take the baking off his hands.

The bakery was on the right of the clock-tower. It had an old-fashioned wood-fuelled oven with a chimney in front over an ash-pit into which the embers were raked, and a separate door to seal the heat inside. Each morning Kurt would remove his shirt and begin by mixing the dough in a great wooden trough, alternately scooping in flour with his right hand and water with his left, until the mixture was a solid, sticky mass. There were sixty pounds of flour in each day's batch, and the last fifteen pounds, to be worked in after the yeast had been added, caused his muscles to ache and the sweat to pour off his chest.

For half an hour the dough remained in the trough to rise while he lit the fire, placing the faggots which had been carefully dried overnight in the oven itself. While the wood burned fiercely enough to produce the necessary heat, he knocked down the dough, punching and kneading it, and then divided and weighed it to form separate, equal loaves. These had to be individually 'turned' so that the surface was smooth and the rough ends were all tucked neatly underneath. This had to be done at top speed or the oven would have cooled too much to bake the bread. At first Kurt found himself painfully slow and Pierre had to come and help in order to get the job done in time, but with a little practice he was able to judge the amount of dough so accurately that he hardly needed the scales, and could double his speed by turning a loaf in each hand.

By the time the bread had been set to rise again, the fire had burned so low that he was able to break up any remaining sticks and rake out the ashes. The oven was now a glowing shell ready to receive the bread. He placed two loaves at a time on a wooden plate at the end of a long pole, swinging them round to deposit them deftly into place. He had to pack the bread to fill the oven exactly, in order to ensure even cooking and also to prevent any dough from being left over, for after a batch had been done the temperature would have fallen too low to bake any more that day.

The whole process called for a high degree of accuracy and timing, but the finished product, with its delicate flavour of wood smoke, was delicious. For Kurt there was the additional reward of the children's unhesitating verdict: the new baker made good bread.

He had no direct contact with the 20 or so boys, except when it was their turn to come and help him wash up, there being a feudal system in operation like an outdated version of that in an English boarding school. This segregated him also from the teaching staff, apart from Pierre and his father, so that he was thrown together with the middle brother, nicknamed Puss, who had greeted him on his arrival and who farmed. The result was that Kurt overlooked certain aims of the school and saw only the ostensible object, that of educating boys in a community that was in close contact with the countryside. He did not find it strange that the boys never went home for the holidays; after all, there could have been no better place than Bassines to evacuate children during the war.

Kurt never got on with Puss, whom he found stand-offish and a bit surly, but there was little alternative in the way of companionship. The two of them had their meals with Georgie van Liefferinge, whose English mother was the matron, and another Jew called George Kluger who had come with M Cougnet from his previous school the year before, and who worked on the land with Puss. Otherwise there was only the boilerman whose wife did the cleaning – an unsatisfactory and none too honest couple – or worse still two filthy, sluttish girls who worked in the kitchen and spoke, in any case, nothing but Walloon.

So Kurt was lonely again, missing his friends in Brussels and rather at a loose end when the day's work was done. His room was no sort of sanctuary: it was in a dilapidated condition, dusty and very damp, and as the sun never penetrated that part of the building, even in midsummer it was permanently cold. The only furniture was the bed, and although Pierre had muttered something about finding a cupboard for him when Kurt had arrived, this had never materialised.

All the same, it proved to be a good thing that he had been given that room. Not long after his arrival he woke in the middle of one night for no apparent reason. There was nothing unusual to hear; it was a dark night and the curtainless window was only a dim square in the opposite wall. As he lay there with his eyes open, wondering what had woken him, something hurtled past his window, landing on the ground with a thud. Very quietly he got up and tried to look out from a position where he could not be detected, but it was too dark to see what had fallen, although he had gained the impression of a fair sized bundle. For a moment he thought he could hear sounds in the room above, where the two girls slept, but as nothing more happened he went back to bed.

Next morning all seemed as it should be, so he kept quiet about the night's activities, until about a week later when he found that he was short of flour. Nor was it for the first time, although on the previous occasions he had thought he had made a mistake in the weighing. This time, however, there was a more noticeable deficit – and also a glaring explanation. Kurt went straight to M Cougnet, reporting the loss of the flour and his suspicions. When examined, the girls' room was found to contain not only the missing flour but a fair amount of other stores, collected ready to be smuggled out through the window and sold on the black market.

The two girls were dismissed on the spot and for a while Pierre Cougnet's wife coped with the cooking. She was small and frail-looking and Kurt found himself spending more time in the kitchen helping with the heavy work. Without the awful cooks this was no hardship, especially now that he was well versed in the bread making and had more time for other jobs. Indeed, he had recently taken over the milling of the flour as well, and as the summer fruit ripened he baked tarts and pastries as well as the daily quota of bread. When a permanent cook arrived he continued these extra duties, for the number of pupils was steadily increasing and a larger staff was needed.

The new cook was Jewish. She was a highly excitable woman of uncertain temper, manipulative and difficult, and Kurt privately wondered why M Cougnet had chosen her. Within a few days of her arrival a nursing sister was engaged also, to take charge of the medical side. She was known as Mme Harris, and Kurt thought that in spite of her extremely youthful appearance she looked every inch a nurse as she bustled about briskly in her crisp uniform. But there, he soon discovered, the professionalism ended. Kurt fell victim to a septic throat and, anxious to return to work as soon as possible, took advice from Mme Harris, who came up with no better cure than to try to open the infected spots. He was not only astonished at such treatment but rendered almost speechless by the torture inflicted. Afterwards, with the benefit of hindsight, he was even more astonished that it never occurred to him at the time to make the simple equation between Mme Harris and his own amateur status at Bassines.

The school was now accepting girl pupils as well, and as Kurt's horizons expanded he began to have more contact with the children. He was surprised at the maturity of the girls compared to the boys, considering that they were presumably of much the same age. With a healthy interest in such matters he noticed that underneath their abbreviated gym slips the girls were all well-developed young women, and what was more that some of them were distinctly interested in him. When the advent of the plum season brought wasps into the kitchen, one of these girls was stung on the calf, and lost no time in running to Kurt for sympathy. Kurt, taken aback by the unnecessary amount he was shown of a very shapely leg, suggested that Mme Harris might be a more effective audience. She wasn't – any more than she had been with Kurt's throat – but even then he never guessed what was going on at Bassines.

Another girl was said to have a boyfriend at the Jewish Committee in Brussels. There were always rumours, as there had been at Marneffe, and as she was one of the more precocious youngsters, Kurt put it all down to high-spirited wishful thinking. But he had under-estimated her: one day she begged a lift in a car going to Brussels in order to meet her young man. The next day Kurt heard from M Cougnet that she had been arrested. She was never heard of again.

M Cougnet was deeply distressed by this. He came to the bakery a few days later while Kurt was clearing up after the morning's work, still looking anxious and depressed. He was sending all the children out on a picnic that afternoon, he said. It was too nice a day to stay indoors doing lessons. Kurt, he thought, could do with a change too. He would like him to accompany them.

Pierre Cougnet was in charge. Having admonished the children that there was to be no shouting and that they must stay close to him, he led the expedition into a thickly-wooded area where they played games until it was time to go home. Kurt, whose senses were sharpened by years of being on the alert for danger, felt a tension among the staff for which he could find no cause. At one point he wandered away by himself until he came within sight of the road. A German jeep was standing at the farm opposite, and as he retreated quickly among the trees, a German motorcyclist roared past.

In that moment he saw everything clearly. He saw why he had his job – and why Mme Harris had hers – and why the cook had been engaged. He went back and looked at the more recent members of the staff with new eyes, and then at some of the children, especially those big little girls putting on their juvenile act. Above all, he recognised the one thing they all had in common with himself that made it imperative that they should be well out of the way when the Germans were known to be present in the neighbourhood. Silently, but with no less gratitude for that, he blessed M Cougnet for his courage and his goodness, from the very depths of his soul.

After that there were many such outings, and Kurt welcomed them not least because they brought him more in contact with the children. During the summer holidays a party of young people visited the school: a youth organisation run by the Liège Electricity Board sent about two dozen children of factory workers to Bassines for a few weeks in the country. Kurt enjoyed their company and even the extra work they made; he was allowed to bake luxuries for them using real white flour which, although his share was only a few more wasp stings, was a pleasure to handle.

Two or three days before these youngsters arrived, the whole school was woken one night by the noise of many aeroplanes. Later, they discovered that the RAF had been caught by waiting Germans on their return from a night raid. As Kurt lay listening to gunfire and bombs at no great distance, there was suddenly a terrific explosion and he found himself on the floor with his bed overturned beside him. In the following silence he realised he had been literally blown out of bed. He got up when he heard shouting outside, and quickly pulling on some clothes, he went to see what was happening.

Several people were milling around in the yard, notably Mme Harris who was shouting hysterically and pointing at the roof – or what was left of it. At one end of the house there was a huge depression with rafters sticking out at grotesque angles like broken bones. Shattered slates were everywhere, and in the middle of it all, unidentifiable from below in the dim light, something was perched – something with a great black rim silhouetted against the sky.

An immediate evacuation of the whole school showed, amazingly, that no one had been hurt, and the children were taken to spend the rest of the night in a barn at a nearby farm. M Cougnet decreed that it was too dangerous for anyone to return until the object on the roof had been declared harmless. This applied to Kurt and the other Jewish members of staff too: there was the unspoken danger also that at first light the Germans would arrive to make an inspection and take control. In the event three of them came. The officer in charge went with Pierre to the top of the house to investigate. An enormous wheel had landed on the roof, smashing through the ceiling of the room below, which, by an incredible stroke of luck, had no one sleeping in it but was being used for storing cupboards during the school holidays.

The men stood speechless in the doorway. The furniture had been robustly made of solid wood; it had been pulverised into unrecognisable splinters. Pierre opened the next door along to assess the extent of the damage. This room appeared to have been quite untouched by the disaster. A small boy who had been unwell and had retired there the day before, in case he had something infectious, was sitting up in bed playing with a tiny brown mouse.

'Look!' he said, 'It's quite tame. It ran in here after that big bang.'

In all the excitement everyone had completely forgotten him.

M Cougnet gave orders that everyone lodged at the farm should remain there until it was safe to return. He used the wheel on the roof as a pretext while there was any chance that it might be a bomb, hoping that the Germans would go away once it had been declared harmless. Unfortunately the situation was more complicated than that. The wheel had belonged to a Halifax bomber which had been shot down, killing two of the crew, and the Germans intended to stay until after their burial. M Cougnet had no option but to bring everyone back to the school and carry on as usual.

The bodies were put in what once had been the private chapel of the château. This was never used by the school because M Cougnet, being a humanist in the best sense, was not a religious man. The Germans on the other hand minded about correct professional etiquette to the point of super-stition. They had shot down hated enemies but they were burying fellow military heroes, and all with equal devotion to duty and lack of personal feeling. The two airmen were laid in state and given full military honours, receiving a great deal more respect than their surviving colleagues who were taken prisoner. The Prussian officer was deeply shocked when the Mayor produced a farm cart to double as a hearse. When it was pointed out to him that it was harvest time and there was no petrol even for the living, he repeated that it was a scandal and that the cart should at the very least be draped entirely in black crepe. Surprise surprise, there was none of that to be had either.

Luckily the Germans were so busy being pompous and keeping their own noses clean that they smelt no rats at the school and asked no awkward questions. Kurt himself had so much to do that there was hardly time to be anxious. He was baking two batches of bread every day and worked with one ear to the Germans, who did not know, of course, that he understood every word they said. Whenever he could relax he escaped from the unbearable reality of life into a good book lent to him by Mme van Liefferinge. At the back of Kurt's mind was still the distant hope that he might yet reach Australia one day, and to this end he sought to improve his English. The school matron had the perfect antidote to stress: Kurt, already an anglophile, now discovered a lifelong delight in the sanity-saving, inconsequential world of P.G. Wodehouse.

The children also found a diversion after their own hearts. When the excitement was over, the surrounding fields were left littered with boxes which the Halifax had ejected before it crashed. Upon investigation these were discovered to contain bomb fuses. Not unnaturally, despite all warnings to leave well alone, the temptation was too great: if they climbed a tree and dropped one, the effect was precisely that of letting off a firework. Even the Germans watched the display with a kind of prim consent bordering on enjoyment. Eventually, however, the children found that some of the bombs were of a different type. These had a red line round them signifying that they were packed with explosives. Miraculously, no one was hurt and after the initial shock these were hailed as an even greater delight, but were quickly forbidden, being altogether too dangerous to be treated as playthings.

When the Germans went away at last, Bassines basked in a halcyon period of relief. Even the children were conscious of a burden lifted; they had grown up with the fear of Germans and could not fail to feel the tension while their presence endured. But for the staff the contrast was unbelievably sweet. Not only had they all been left in peace but an uncanny sense of security prevailed. The Germans had seen nothing amiss, nothing to make them suspicious. Bassines had been checked and passed and would be in the clear for a long time to come.

There was a holiday mood: when the young people from Liège arrived they celebrated with a singsong round a camp fire, to which Kurt and some of the resident pupils were invited. At first they went through a repertory of French songs which became more and more patriotic in flavour until they graduated to Dutch and other languages where a pro-English verse or two was known by someone. It was a marvellous excuse for vocal flag-waving and the children gave full vent to the shedding of inhibitions normally imposed upon them.

Light headed with the glorious sense of freedom from Germans, Kurt struck up with 'Tipperary'. He sang it loudly and with great gusto until suddenly he was aware that he sang alone. After the first few notes the children had realised that the words were English. There was dead silence in the

audience as 30 or so faces stared at him, mesmerised by what
they heard. Kurt struggled on bravely to the end of the verse,
and then his voice too petered out. In the hush that followed
he could hear whispering round the central glow of the fire.

'Who is he?'

'He must be English!'

The visiting children had been regaled endlessly with the
tale of the English plane, and had not met Kurt before that
evening. Rumours rapidly spread that he had been on the
plane – that he was a spy dropped by the English. The alle-
gations had such terrifying associations for Kurt, even coming
from children's lips, that he looked quickly towards M
Cougnet for support. To his amazement, the headmaster
hesitated, almost as if he were not prepared to deny what had
been said. Then he leaned forward.

'No, no, children!' He sounded as startled as Kurt felt.
'This gentleman is not a spy. He is – er – he's our baker, of
course! Aren't you? Tell them!' he hissed at Kurt.

'No – I mean, yes,' Kurt stammered. 'I mean, I am not a
spy!' he insisted vehemently.

'How are things in England?' called out one intrepid voice
from the darkness. Others took up the theme.

'How is London?'

'I have no idea – I've never been there!'

They nudged each other, whispering. Of course he would
have to say that. Clearly, they did not believe him for a
moment. Then M Cougnet rose to his feet and when he spoke
he sounded very grave.

'Listen everybody – we've had enough of this now. This
gentleman is the school baker. Is that clearly understood?
Now, I want no more talk of this sort to anyone. It could be
very dangerous, very dangerous indeed. Come, shake hands
with the baker, and promise me not to say another word
about tonight.'

Obediently, they promised. Then they shook hands with
Kurt, the excitement of conspiracy shining from their eyes in
the last glow of the firelight. Later, he tumbled to it. M
Cougnet had taken advantage of the children's mistake and

was using it for everyone's protection. They would honour their promise of silence without any idea of the secret they were really keeping.

When the visiting children had left, Kurt moved into a much better room on the upper floor of what had once been the stables. The lower part of the building was converted into classrooms above which was a long dormitory and a single bedroom each for Kurt and Georgie van Liefferinge. At about the same time that Kurt moved into more salubrious quarters it became necessary for the grain store to do so too. Kurt arrived one day to start milling and found that he was not alone: there in front of him sat the biggest rat that he had ever seen. When it saw Kurt it made for a hole in the corner, only to find that it was so gorged with grain that it could not get out of the store. For the split second that they confronted each other, it would have been hard to say which was the more frightened. The rat looked extremely aggressive, and whereas Kurt was unprepared for battle, the rat was armed to the teeth. Kurt gave the loathsome creature the victory and fled, slamming the door behind him.

The large resident tomcat was very surprised to have his siesta disturbed by a problem which was considered his department. He was even more surprised by the sight that met his eyes when Kurt pushed him through the barely opened granary door. A moment later he shot out again, long before he and the rat had begun to get acquainted. There being nothing else for it, Kurt fetched a poker and, gritting his teeth, settled the matter himself.

After that it was out of the question to continue storing the grain there. The cellars, although ideal for keeping wine, were too damp for other purposes, so Kurt went with Pierre to investigate the loft as an alternative. They used a back staircase emerging into a narrow passage with panelled rooms on either side. Pierre beckoned Kurt into one of them and counted the panels along one of the walls. He pressed the next panel and to Kurt's amazement it swung open, revealing a small inner room which had been entirely invisible before. When Kurt had counted the number of panels for himself, Pierre closed the door again without a word. As no explanation was offered, Kurt said nothing either. The secret room had been furnished with a table, on which stood a typewriter, and the absence of dust on both led him to suppose that the place was often used.

Further along the passage Pierre tried another room with a view to storing grain, this time with totally unexpected results for them both. In the centre was a pile of books reaching nearly to the ceiling. When the château had ceased to be a private house someone had cleared the library and moved the books up here. Half of Kurt wanted to sing out loud with joy at stumbling upon such a treasure trove; the other half could have wept at the state in which he found it. The books had been chucked higgledy-piggledy into the loft like refuse on a rubbish tip. There were Latin and Greek parchments, first editions of classics, whole series of beautiful leather-bound volumes with tooled gold lettering on the bindings, ancient copies of much-loved favourites and books which had been inscribed more than a hundred years before. Neglect had done its worst; there was a musty smell and mildew lay in a grey film over everything. Kurt picked up an anthology of poetry; the loose pages cracked and crumbled in his hand while the once splendid morocco cover flaked into layers between his fingers. Oblivious of everything else, he still sat on top of the heap long after Pierre had gone downstairs again, inspecting, reading, sorting and absorbing, until at last it grew too dark to read the print before him.

Once it had been emptied, the loft made an ideal place to store grain. With M Cougnet's permission Kurt transported every book still worthy of the name downstairs, until the heap had dwindled to nothing but a few sheets of torn scrap paper on the bare boards. Then he set about lining the walls of his room with the volumes in the best condition. The children were at first intrigued, then fascinated, then so fired with enthusiasm that there were dozens of offers of good homes for the books Kurt could not house. A room competition was launched and after an active week of excited secrecy an open day was held when everyone was invited to admire everyone else's creative decor.

The original effects produced by some of the children were impressive, especially considering the paucity of scope and materials. The finished designs varied surprisingly, although all of them displayed the same mix of ancient and modern: every room had amassed as many shelves of old books as possible, and these jockeyed for position with abstract sculptures in metal, all of which had once been parts of a Halifax bomber. But there was one feature which seemed to be *de rigueur*, from Kurt's own room down to the dormitory of the most junior pupils: all the book ends were identical cylindrical canisters, of which the most prized had a red stripe round them.

Kurt developed his room into his home. By day his bed became a sofa with the help of a couple of cushions, and the secretary had provided him with two beautiful Rodin prints which now adorned his walls. It marked the beginning of a new era for him at Bassines, a broadening not only of friendships but of all his activities. An old friend of M Cougnet's came to stay to bottle fruit for the establishment during the winter. Kurt, a compulsive cleaner of saucepans, did the washing up for her, earning not only her thanks but her interest in his presence there. He was already much in demand teaching bridge to the older children, and now, when it came out that he was a graduate in economics, he was pressed into service as an instructor in that too, thus becoming involved in every sphere of activity at the château.

With the possible exception of the aggrieved tomcat, even the animals enjoyed a period of unprecedented attention not afforded them in more harassed times. At the back of the house, where there had once been lawns and a formal garden, there were now crops growing and pasture for a goat and a few sheep. Puss, Georgie and George Kluger tended these and milked the goat, making a valuable contribution to the children's diet. Food was scarce throughout Belgium, but especially so at Bassines where more and more of the pupils and staff were Jews in hiding, and therefore had no official existence and no ration books.

The goat ran around free, so confident of her worth to the community that her head became lamentably turned and she had the effrontery to fall in love with Georgie. For most of the time she followed him about harmlessly enough, but Georgie liked playing football at weekends, and when he absented himself the goat became quite desperate. Unless every door was firmly shut, the brazen hussy would get in and find her way to Georgie's room, compensating for her deprivation by eating everything in her path. The sheep posed an entirely different problem. The ram had to be kept tethered, being, as Kurt had good reason to know, extremely vicious. One evening he had agreed to shut up the animals for Georgie, and had failed to persuade either the ram or the ewes to go through the gate first, as the ewes lacked the necessary initiative and the ram was too jealous to leave his ewes alone with Kurt. Eventually Kurt himself had had to lead the way into the pen, whereupon the ram had seized his opportunity and butted his well-meaning escort black and blue.

On another occasion the ram got loose and walked into the yard, causing wholesale consternation as everyone present jumped for the nearest door and hid inside. In two minutes flat the ram found himself alone in the yard, apart from a little trailer – and the goat, who seemed supremely unconcerned. The ram reminded her of her manners by butting her, and the goat retaliated in kind. The dialogue was repeated until the goat discovered that if she jumped onto the cart, not only was she out of reach but the ram banged his head against the trailer. This was so satisfactory that she got down from her pedestal and taught him the same lesson again... and again... After about the fourth time the ram was charging the trailer in such a rage that the force of the impact left him blinded with pain, while his head was bleeding freely. Eventually four strong men had to remove him bodily before he killed himself, while the goat watched triumphantly from her superior position of safety. Kurt could have sworn he saw her smiling.

For a while it had been a happy time at Bassines, but like all idylls it was much too good to last.

It came to an end abruptly one day in the autumn of 1942. M Cougnet was out, and Kurt, having completed the day's baking, was resting in the kitchen when George Kluger rushed in shouting, 'Kurt! Germans!' He was gone by the time Kurt was on his feet.

Kurt ran outside to see George heading for the woods beyond the boundary, and had already started to follow him before common sense caught up with instinct, making him turn back. The Germans had not necessarily come to make an arrest: all kinds of petty officialdom could have brought them to the château. To be seen running away would only throw suspicion on himself and George and possibly on the whole of Bassines. Mlle Bernaert, the secretary, had gone out to the Germans in the hope, no doubt, of keeping them from coming any further. Kurt could hear her shouting for George Kluger; evidently, then, they had asked for him, and George, heeding the secretary's warning as intended, had run away.

Kurt went back to the bakery where there was a good view of the German truck while he himself remained out of the way. All the same, he was too close for comfort. He would be intensely vulnerable if the Germans made a search for George and started asking questions. His mind sought desperately for an excuse to leave the château which would seem reasonable if he were accosted.

For a while he watched and waited, summoning his nerve and hoping to see the Germans give up and go away before he had to move. But the truck remained in the yard and he could only assume that they were still looking for George. He decided to go before they emerged from the château; there was no knowing what they might do next and it would look suspicious if he started to leave just as they came his way. He walked slowly past the waiting German driver, aware of the watching eyes on the back of his head, and went into the secretary's office. She looked up in surprise: two of the Germans were in there while the others searched the premises.

'Excuse me,' said Kurt steadily, 'I'm just going to the blacksmith's for the implements he's been mending. Do you want anything from the village?'

She understood. 'No thank you.'

He walked out of the office, out of the château and then out of the gate in the direction of the village, forcing himself to move casually and not to look back to see if the Germans were watching him. There was a footpath through the fields which was secluded except for the place where it crossed the main road. Here it was necessary to walk along the open highway for a few hundred yards before the path was resumed on the other side. Kurt stopped, breathing deeply. He was tempted to hide at the farm on the corner, but if anybody were to see him it might arouse suspicion and call into question his own legal status.

He decided to go on, praying fervently that he might not meet with the Germans at the exact moment that they finished at the château and passed that way themselves. It was long odds, given such a short stretch of road and such uncertain timing, but it was a meeting that was too dreadful to contemplate. He knew that by all the laws of chance it should not happen, but a sixth sense told him that it would.

The truck came up behind him when he was precisely midway along the road. From the moment that he first heard the engine he was in no doubt who it was, and in the next few seconds he debated his chances of survival. To run or not to run... If he ran, he was automatically guilty; if he stayed, they had him. To be or not to be. If he made a break for it, he had to reach the woods before they caught him. If he just walked on, they could pick him up then and there. He made up his mind to run. But it was already too late: they were drawing level with him now.

Kurt walked on, his eyes with his hopes in the gutter, pleading even as he heard the brakes squeal, At least let them not stop. They stopped.

'George Kluger?'

'No!'

'Who are you?'

By what seemed quite gratuitously ill fortune, the Belgian boy whose identity card he had shared the same first name. 'George...' Kurt began.

Immediately the guns were pointing in his direction. His heart plummeted into his trousers. Any minute now the German officer would ask to see his identity card, on which the photograph did not tally with his appearance. Kurt's instinct was to remain one jump ahead, with what would seem to be innocent co-operation. The identity card formed a triptych with the photograph in the middle; Kurt put his hand in his pocket and brought the card out folded, showing the Germans only the page on which was written plainly the owner's name and the fact that he was Belgian.

The officer looked at it and then waved him away with a disdainful hand. The guns were lowered. The driver started up the engine. They drove on out of sight along the road. As soon as his knees had stopped trembling Kurt turned round and walked back to Bassines. After all, he had no idea how to find the blacksmith anyway.

It was a relief to tell his experience to the secretary, and later to M Cougnet. They reassured him that George Kluger would be quite equal to the situation, knowing the neighbourhood and the local farmers well. George himself put Kurt's mind at rest by reappearing that night and coming to Kurt's room. He was with good friends, he said. He took some clothes and returned to the farm where he was hiding.

Kurt discussed all this with M Cougnet two or three times, until he was asked not to do so any more because it was becoming too dangerous. The boilerman was not to be trusted, M Cougnet told him, and was getting suspicious of the baker's frequent contact with management. Kurt suggested a one-act play for the boilerman's benefit: M Cougnet was to come in when he knew they were together and tear Kurt off a strip, telling him to stop interfering over George Kluger and reminding him of his position. M Cougnet displayed such a talent for acting that the shock was almost genuine, and was so convincingly explosive that the boilerman sided with Kurt when they were alone again. Bosses were all the same, he sympathised, rotten through and through when you saw them in their true colours. When Kurt told him about it, M Cougnet was absolutely delighted.

But these little triumphs were of only temporary duration, while the perpetual shadow was never far away. In spite of the shortage of transport and petrol, even for the Germans at that stage of the war, they had already sent a military vehicle with six men to arrest one sixteen-year-old boy who was the only Jew officially on the register at Bassines. Kurt knew too that people in hiding sometimes used the school for one or two nights at a time, and he had not forgotten the little room at the top of the house behind the secret panel. If the Germans got wind of these things, or that there were more Jews about the place (and there were plenty by now at Bassines) they might at any moment, day or night, be back. If they searched the premises, Kurt for one had several incriminating documents to warrant his arrest and deportation.

One evening soon after George Kluger's escape he looked out his University Degree, his Matura Certificate, his Certificate of Tailoring and one or two other papers bearing his real name, and sealed them in a biscuit tin. Then he went for a walk and threw the tin onto a rubbish tip near one of the neighbouring farms. He hoped that this way they might survive the ravages of war and weather so that one day he could retrieve them, but he never saw them again.

In the autumn two girls who were genuine teachers came to Bassines: Marcelle, who lived near Huy, taught the primary school age; Marie-Thérèse, who was trained to teach grammar school children, came from Liège. Kurt and Georgie formed a foursome with the girls, spending evenings and any available free time at weekends together with them. There was very little leisure for Kurt. He soon found himself urgently needed as a translator into German. Many young Belgians from farming families were being sent to work in Germany, and it had been found that if the applications to have them exempted were written in German, they stood a much better chance of success. Kurt worked willingly at this, often late into the night, M Cougnet insisting that the Underground would have liked to pay him for it. Kurt, of course, refused, and M Cougnet replied prophetically that perhaps the time would come when they could do something for him.

Kurt's days were taken up with preserving fruit and vegetables for the months ahead. M Cougnet had managed to buy a large quantity of plums from local growers so that the children should have a source of vitamin C in the winter. There was no sugar, of course: they were bottled with chemical preservatives and consequently tasted very sour indeed. An enormous crop of cabbages came up at the château, which had to be salted and stored in the cellars in stone compartments. Kurt developed the biceps of an all-in wrestler chopping cabbages for hours on end, until he felt he never wanted to look at the stuff again.

The food was monotonous and not very appetising, and in spite of every effort to give the children particularly enough to eat, it was extremely scanty and everyone was perpetually hungry. Kurt had been away from home for five years now and had suffered undernourishment for longer than the rest, resulting all at once in his teeth starting to go bad. The first time this made itself felt, M Cougnet sent him to Ciney where a dentist carried out two extractions. It was not an experience he would have chosen, but compared with the next time that it became necessary, the first occasion seemed in retrospect like a celebration.

He was aware of it when he woke up one morning, a familiar twinge which came and occasionally went – as long as he remembered not to bite on it. He said nothing because he knew it was too dangerous to make the journey to Ciney again: the Germans had stepped up their press-ganging activities and he was in just the right age group to attract their notice with a view to forced labour in Germany. Throughout the day the periods of respite from pain grew shorter and fewer until it became continuous and eating was out of the question. By the evening he was holding a handkerchief soaked in cold water to his jaw, his face now noticeably swollen and the pain all-pervasive.

He spent a sleepless night, kept awake not only by toothache but by the hopelessness of the situation. It had come at a particularly bad moment: the Germans were having a bout of raiding local farms for young men just such as himself, making it dangerous to go out at all, let alone to travel to Ciney. By morning his whole head was throbbing and his face was as puffy and tender as if he had mumps. It was impossible to go on any longer. He went to M Cougnet and told him that even risking capture by the Germans would be preferable to what he was enduring.

M Cougnet was deeply sympathetic, having had toothache himself only the week before. He studied Kurt's outsized, ashen face for a minute in silence and then he agreed that something would have to be done. He undertook that if Kurt could bear it for a little longer he would arrange for a plan to be worked out. The mere promise of relief worked like an analgesic, and Kurt went straight to the bakery, preferring to keep as busy as possible rather than to have time to dwell on his affliction.

He never knew how he got through the next couple of days. At some stage he remembered being given his instructions by M Cougnet for the following morning, and at four o'clock he had to creep out to meet one of the local people at the gate. From here he was guided the long way round through the woods to the village. Every few hundred yards there was a sentinel with a cigarette lighter; he waited for a signal from the next man that all was clear, then stumbled on again in the dark. The last man led him to the door of a darkened house. With the Germans so much in evidence, the blackout was minutely observed and there was not a thread of light to be seen anywhere. His escort knocked softly a couple of times and then melted like a ghost into the night.

The terrified dentist who admitted Kurt was well aware, under the circumstances, that his victim was some kind of hot potato. His hands were shaking as he pointed to the surgery and indicated to Kurt to get up onto the chair. He was in such a panic to get the visit over and be rid of his dangerous patient that he did not stop for an examination, nor did he administer any anaesthetic; he merely pulled a tooth at random from the grossly inflamed gum offered to him, followed by its neighbour, to be, he divulged in a hoarse whisper, on the safe side. In the aftermath of relief not yet unmixed with agony, Kurt comforted himself with the dubious satisfaction of a rare experience: it is not every day that the dentist is more frightened than his patient.

The toothache, for the moment at any rate, was over, but it was only the beginning of a long period of associated ill health. The winter was hard, and not made any easier by the poor quality food, and a serious lack of that. Spring brought no alleviation, being still bitterly cold and wet with an east wind that shrivelled all it touched. The caterers at Bassines had managed to buy a consignment of brown beans of doubtful origin, in the hope of adding some cheap protein to the meals. The intention proved better than the results for the beans had been meant for pig food, and soon afterwards one of the children became seriously ill with diarrhoea. He ran such a high temperature with these symptoms that the local doctor was frightened into thinking that it might be typhoid, and ordered everyone on the premises to be vaccinated immediately. This involved two injections in the shoulder blade; after the first, Kurt's shoulder was so stiff and swollen that he had considerable difficulty kneading the dough, while the second laid him out completely.

For a few days he felt too ill to care very much whether he lived or died. When he began to mend, the fears and anxieties which never retreated very far crept back to haunt his mind and hinder his recovery. He had no wish for food – certainly not for anything available to him – and sat quietly in his room sipping *tisanne* and worrying about what he would do if the Germans came while he was in his present weak state.

Indeed, Bassines was necessarily so wrapped up in its own health problems that when the Germans were again seen to be active in the neighbourhood, M Cougnet became concerned about security. He arranged for all the men to take turns in pairs acting as night watchmen in the woods. A long line of wire was connected to a bell which rang in the house, and although it was a more or less Heath Robinson contraption, when Kurt and Georgie did a shift they felt safer than they would have done had there been no warning at all.

To his aching shoulder Kurt now added severe stomach pains. These were bad enough for M Cougnet to call the doctor, whose diagnosis was that Kurt probably had ulcers. He was put on a strict diet of milk and was told that he should have an X-ray if such a thing could be arranged. It so happened that Marie-Thérèse had a sister who was a medical student at the hospital in Liège, and she invited Kurt to her parents' house while he had this done. This stroke of luck, however, did not mean that the whole undertaking would be plain sailing. Travelling at that time was almost impossibly difficult; no-one could tell when trains would run or how long they would take, and for Kurt there was the added fear that there would certainly be Germans on every railway station and train, all of them on the watch for people just such as himself.

But the biggest snag of all threatened to prevent him from even getting started. To attend the hospital he had to have valid papers, and the ones he had would not stand up to the inevitable scrutiny. He had not reckoned, however, with the local Underground movement and their recognition of the time and trouble he had spent in translation. Because of this, M Cougnet felt able to approach them, and they provided Kurt with a new identity card. So Kurt Pick became Philippe Georges Kurth Koninck, thus retaining the name by which he was known and his genuine initials if anyone saw a monogram on his clothes or possessions. He also had his own photograph and date of birth on his new papers, although these now showed that he was a Belgian citizen whose birthplace had been Ostende, the extensive bombing there having conveniently destroyed all previous records of his existence.

As a bonus, whereas his old papers had been registered in Brussels, his new ones were registered at Bassines, thus placing him as a *bona fide* local whose presence at the school would be likely to raise far fewer eyebrows among the German authorities.

The journey to Liège and back, although lengthy and uncomfortable, was otherwise without incident. There was even a certain pleasurable excitement about escaping from the narrow confines of the school. The X-rays showed no ulcers. He might almost have considered that the whole exercise had been for nothing, except that through it he had acquired a valuable new identity – disposing of the old one, of course, through the usual channels.

The deprivations of war took their toll not only in health but in the petty resentments and bickering among the staff at Bassines. With such a diversity of backgrounds among the Jewish domestics, Kurt could not altogether escape the jealousy caused by his advancement into so many extra-curricular activities, nor the peevish innuendoes from some of the cleaners. He was aware of tensions over what they saw as his unfairly privileged position, and heard murmurs to the effect that he was not the only one to feel unwell. Added to that, they told him in no uncertain terms that he worked much too hard, the reasoning behind this solicitude being that it showed up their efforts in a bad light. He would have only himself to blame, they warned him, if the Germans came and he found himself too weak to run away. Kurt assured them that he would manage somehow, but afterwards, in the depression of convalescence, he was haunted by the very doubts that they had raised.

Several times after that he was called upon to prove it. Whenever there was an alert because Germans had been seen in the vicinity, M Cougnet found some excuse, such as a nature walk, to get everyone off the premises. On one occasion when they were hiding in some bushes outside the grounds, Kurt had stayed on longer than the others, suspicious that it was not yet safe to return. It was almost dusk by the time he went upstairs to his room, weak with fatigue, but his relief to find that life had returned to normal again was short-lived. As he undressed for bed he discovered that he no longer had his precious identity card with him.

He slipped out in the fading light, wondering desperately how he would remember which way he had taken in the earlier scramble. Then, while he retraced his footsteps to the gate into the woods, childhood memories of Karl May's stories of trappers came sharply to his mind, and he began to search for long forgotten clues that would lead him along the right path. Slowly but surely, here observing a snapped twig, there a shoe-print in the earth, he tracked his way back to the thicket where he had lain hidden. There was still a slight depression in the grass following the curve of his body, in the centre of which lay a small piece of folded card exactly as it must have fallen when he had risen from the spot.

In spite of all M Cougnet's precautions, by the time summer came Bassines was hardly a safe place any longer. More and more Jews were being secretly absorbed into its structure, increasing the danger of discovery for everyone and reducing the amount of food available to each person. While physically surviving became more of a problem, the necessity to camouflage this situation increased in proportion, for the good will that the school had enjoyed from the Germans at the time of the crashed plane had long since expired and the occupying forces were tightening their grip on every sphere of life.

M Cougnet started taking large parties of children and staff to church every Sunday as part of a drive to conceal the preponderance of Jewish residents. All the same – or perhaps even because of such deceptions – Marie-Thérèse's father guessed M Cougnet's underlying purposes and became worried for her safety. He found her a job in Liège, believing that the disadvantages of town life were now more acceptable than the risks his daughter was running in the country, and shortly afterwards Marie-Thérèse left the school and went home to her parents.

At five o'clock one morning her father's worst fears were realised for those who remained at Bassines.

Kurt, in a deep sleep at last after a restless night, was aware of someone bursting into his room with the news that the Germans were in the yard. At first he thought he was dreaming the familiar nightmare that the Gestapo had come in the night with his name on a deportation order; he could hear the staccato voices shouting, 'Raus! Raus! Raus!' and the stamping jackboots in the yard.

He sat up in a sweat of fright to shake the hideous sounds from his consciousness, only to find that he could still hear them now that he was thoroughly awake. Doors banged, someone cried out in panic, the younger children were screaming and over everything was the incessant barking of orders and the tramping of military feet. People were running along the passage, disorganised and bewildered, pulling on clothes as they passed Kurt's door. He started to struggle to his feet but a dizzy weakness overcame him and he lurched back onto his bed. The frightened cries had ceased now, to be replaced by the silence of terror.

The next moment a German soldier appeared in Kurt's doorway, ordering him out into the passage. Kurt said that he was ill, fear and pain gripping his guts. But the man was armed and there was no option but to submit to being chased out at gun-point to join Georgie and the children where they stood petrified on the landing.

In the taut silence they shuffled downstairs and were herded into the main building, the only sound coming from the Germans prodding them along with their ceaseless 'Raus! Raus! Raus!'

At the bottom of the back stairs Kurt checked for an instant. If he disentangled himself from the group he might escape up there to the little panelled sanctuary where he could hide until it was all over. Surely it had been for just this emergency that Pierre had shown him the secret room... He stepped to one side, glancing round him: there were no Germans watching and he could dash upstairs and be round the corner before anyone realised he had gone – unless, of course, the passage above was guarded, and that he did not know. To run headlong into a German up there would be worse than staying where he was. Once again he debated whether to run or to stay. He decided that the risk of meeting a patrolling German was too great, and went on with the others.

He was shoved into the main entrance hall which was usually a recreation room, where he found himself pinned behind a couple of tables with the other male members of staff. The ghastly shouting in German added to the prisoners' apprehension; Kurt, still wearing his pyjamas, found that he was shivering, while the man next to him was literally jabbering under his breath with fright.

Presently two German officers came into the hall. It was clear from a few preliminary questions of a general nature that everyone was about to be interrogated. Kurt's instinctive reaction was to get his turn over as quickly as possible, knowing that the longer he had to wait, the less capable he would be of giving the impression that he had nothing to fear. Like all bullies, the Germans would spot any weakness instantly, and his stomach was already cramped with tension and pain. He would fare worse if he appeared too sick with terror to stand up by himself. So while the others with him shuffled and gazed at their shoes, he deliberately caught the eye of one of the officers and managed to force a confident half smile. The result was immediately successful: he was singled out to be the first for questioning.

He gave his name and produced his identity papers showing that his job was *surveillant* at the school. He was ill, hence the pyjamas, and needed a diet of milk which was only obtainable at Bassines. After a few more questions he was sent to the other end of the room, drooping with the strain of his ordeal. Instantly, M Cougnet was at his elbow, murmuring encouragement and characteristically backing up his plea of sickness by ordering a chair to be brought. Someone obliged, and for the remaining inquisition Kurt sat there limply, an incongruous figure in his pyjamas, lolling in a deckchair.

The interrogations were detailed and continued for some time. A few of the men were ordered to join Kurt across the room; most were taken out to the waiting transport. When this was over those who remained were sent back to their rooms.

Having pleaded illness, Kurt determined to adhere rigidly to this, and lay on his bed while he waited for something more to happen. He waited a long time, pain and anxiety gnawing at his stomach, for the brooding silence was almost more unnerving than the earlier noise had been. Once or twice he crept to the edge of the window, hoping to catch a glimpse of what was going on, but he could see nothing except that the German trucks still stood in the yard.

Hours later the door was suddenly flung open, revealing an armed soldier who demanded loudly to know what Kurt was doing there, and shouted at him to get out. Kurt replied that he had been told to stay there, which called forth the shrill command: 'Out! Out, you dirty Jew!'

Stung by the adjective, Kurt's denial was emphatic, but the soldier was looking for trouble. He repeated his accusation in a variety of terms, coming into the room and surveying its contents. All at once he caught sight of a print Kurt had on his wall of *La Source* by Ingres. It was a charming little picture of a nude girl, innocently romantic, and Kurt loved the touch of beauty it brought to the austerity of his quarters.

The German leered at it, his eyes gleaming with prurient lust. It was disgusting, he declared; only a filthy Jew would have dirty pictures of naked women in his bedroom. He tore his gaze from it and turned to the only other picture on display – a photograph of Kurt's parents. The sight of this released from his mouth a contaminated torrent of anti-semitism, leaving Kurt astonished that such unoriginal insults could be so degrading to them both. When the soldier had run out of terms of abuse he had Kurt out of bed and drove him at gunpoint downstairs and into the corridor outside the dining-room. This time there was no opportunity to double back up the other staircase to the secret room, and Kurt regretted bitterly that he had not risked meeting a guard at the top and gone when the chance had been offered.

He was handed over to another soldier and found himself in the company of several of the older pupils. A quick glance round, coupled with his inside knowledge of Bassines, showed him that he had one thing in common with all these boys. He spoke to the German, hoping to draw his attention away from this onto himself for a different reason.

'Malade,' he said. One of the boys promptly translated this into German for the soldier's benefit. He was the cook's son, a dark, curly-headed boy, very Jewish looking. The soldier glanced at him sharply, and then, more sympathetically, at Kurt. 'What illness?'

Kurt had decided that, as far as the Germans were concerned, he had cancer. There was no need to pretend the pain and he suspected he looked grey enough to fool anyone. Grimacing a little, he indicated that it was in his stomach and that he had it very badly. The cook's son told the soldier in German what he had said, and then relayed the reply back to Kurt in French. The soldier was mildly sympathetic: pain was no fun, he said; he himself had toothache. The irony of the boy interpreting for them when his own native tongue was French was not lost on Kurt, but his amusement was short-lived. The dining-room door was flung open and the cook's son was summoned inside for further interrogation. Kurt knew that it was only a short step from there to the waiting transport, which inevitably spelt disaster. The boy's real name was Rubinstein and his father had been one of the greatest chess players the world has ever known.

Presently the door opened again, and this time it was Kurt who was admitted to the dining-room. Two officers stood in front of the table and the inevitable questions began again: 'Are you a Jew? Show your identity card! What are you doing here?'

Kurt tried to look resigned, even bored by it all. No, he was not a Jew, he was ill with a very serious stomach complaint. The officer resorted to bulldozing tactics: No! He was lying! He was a Jew!

They argued the point stubbornly, Kurt gritting his teeth while the German tried to wear him down with endless repetitious questions. Why in the world, he wondered, did they not order him to recite the Lord's Prayer and have done with it?

'If you are ill, we have doctors in Germany...'

Kurt insisted that it was not doctors he needed, it was milk. The officers grew impatient; they started to hit him in the face after every answer. Kurt, so exhausted now that he almost wished to get into one of the waiting trucks and make an end of everything, retorted roughly that it was all very well for them, but he didn't think them very brave when he couldn't hit back. For a moment he thought they were going to kill him then and there, but they merely pressed their advantage as they saw him beginning to weaken. He was a Jew; they knew he was a Jew! They spat the words till they rang in Kurt's ears, and he answered them over and over again, 'Non! Non! Non!'

The voices came and went now. He was losing track of where he was and how long he had been there, swaying a little on his feet as his head began to feel muzzy from the blows. He knew he was getting to the end of his tether; it would not take much more of this before they broke him and he gave himself away. The time had come to finish this whole business one way or the other.

'Look here!' he shouted. 'If I were a Jew I would have been circumcised, wouldn't I?' Desperately, and without stopping to consider what would happen if they called his bluff, he began to unbutton his pyjamas, insisting that they could see for themselves whether he was speaking the truth.

The scandalised Germans quickly turned their faces away from this outrage.

'Get out!'

On his way back to his room Kurt met the soldier who had brought him from it.

'You are a filthy Jew...' the man began. Kurt stopped and looked him straight in the face. 'On the contrary,' he replied, 'your officer has just cleared me. And if you don't believe me, you can go and ask him yourself.'

155

He woke next morning to a gentle knocking on his door and the presence of two figures in his room. They were not Germans – that much was certain – and he then saw that they were both women. He remembered lying on his bed the day before while the afternoon dragged on into eternity, listening for something more to happen. At last there had been more noise, not of shouting this time, but the sound of coming and going, the slamming of car doors and endless striding feet. After that there had been blessed silence, and he had drifted off into an uneasy, restless sleep.

His visitors now were both members of staff. Their eyes were ringed with lack of sleep and Kurt could guess that any news they brought was not encouraging. He learned that the guard had been replaced by old soldiers who had been put in to hold the fort. These were so frightened by a possible attack by the *Maquis* that they had barricaded themselves into the main building with the remaining children, having first pillaged the precious stores of food – melting down anything that contained fat to send home to Germany.

The worst news was yet to come. Kurt heard in silence that the whole Cougnet family had been arrested and taken away. The three of them discussed in frightened whispers how they might escape, not knowing what else might have happened nor who might be around to hear them. Then one of the girls reported that she had been given permission to go to the dentist later that morning without further questioning.

It occurred to Kurt that there would be no harm in trying the same formula himself. He dressed and went down to the main hall and approached the soldier in charge. He was very ill, he said, and had been sent to Bassines because of the special care and diet of milk available to him there. The only future for him now was to go into hospital. Once he realised Kurt's objective, the German lost interest and merely asked as a formality which hospital. Kurt told him that it was the General Hospital in Namur, Liège being in the opposite direction.

The soldier gave his consent and Kurt packed a suitcase and shortly afterwards he walked away from Bassines for the last time. One of the boys carried his luggage, as befitted a sick man, and someone telephoned a nearby farmer to ask him to come with his van. Not unnaturally, the man was afraid to come too close, but he agreed to wait for Kurt at the end of the wood. As soon as they were out of sight of the German guards Kurt asked his driver to take him to the station.

Here he found the secretary, who had just arrived on a train from Brussels, returning to the school after a few days off duty. She had heard from the station-master that the Gestapo had raided the château and was glad to see Kurt. She listened eagerly to his account of events and decided to turn right round and go home again on the next train. As if to confirm her decision, at that moment a group of boys from Bassines sped past the station on bicycles, among them the lad who had carried Kurt's case. Evidently, he had taken the hint and they had all escaped while the going was good. Kurt's relief as he watched them go was tempered by the absence of young Rubinstein from their company. He could only draw the worst conclusions about what had happened to him.

Presently the telephone rang in the station-master's office. Kurt and Mlle Bernaert, suspicious that the call came from Bassines, strained their ears to hear what was being said. It was obviously a German on the other end, but whether the same men were still in charge or whether the Gestapo had returned to take over again, they could not tell. They heard the station-master saying that there were no passengers waiting, and when he had rung off he came out onto the platform. He indicated a little incline where there was a house with a balcony commanding a good view of the road leading to the station. He gave a shout and a woman appeared on the balcony. The station-master called to her to shake a white sheet if she saw an approaching car. If the Germans came looking for them, he told the two companions, she would warn them so that they could hide.

The train for Huy hardly came to a halt. As he clambered in Kurt caught a glimpse of the station-master speaking briefly to the driver. Then he began to worry wretchedly whether the Germans would be there waiting for him at the next station... or the next... Or if the station-master had failed to convince them on the telephone, it would be the easiest thing in the world for them to have a reception committee waiting for him at Huy. He spent a great deal of the journey in the lavatory, his heart seizing up every time the train slowed down. Just short of Huy, he felt the brakes being applied. He looked out of the window cautiously; the train had stopped on a quiet, unfenced stretch of line running alongside the road. Realising what the station-master had said to the driver, Kurt jumped down and walked across the track. As soon as he was clear, the train moved on again.

He was in the town by the time a German car drew level with him. He stopped, partly because there was a shop window to gaze into, averting his face, and partly because his legs were suddenly threatening to buckle under him. The reflection in the glass showed him that the car was slowing down and that the men in it were officers. They stopped. It was all horribly familiar – and this time he was stuck with the incriminating suitcase in his hand. He stared with everything that was in him at the objects in the window – and then the traffic went on, and the German car with it. Kurt continued slowly along the road without the faintest idea what sort of shop it had been.

To get to the station for a train to Liège, he had to cross the river. There was only one bridge and this, of course, was guarded by an alert-looking German soldier. It seemed to Kurt by now that the whole world was on the lookout for him, and that the soldier was bound to have explicit instructions to arrest him on the spot. He ambled out of sight round a corner, put down the suitcase and began to think out what he would say when he was stopped. He thought about it for a long time, but neither the excuse presented itself, nor did Kurt feel any more ready to face the music; nor, when he crept round the corner from time to time to take a look, had the guard gone away. But he could not stay there: this was a particularly bad town in which to be stuck after curfew. The offices of the

Area *Kommandantur* were in Huy, and would be bound to know about the raid on Bassines. The place was a hornets' nest of Germans, and the longer he stayed the more likely he was to get stung.

Eventually he picked up the suitcase again, and with the other hand firmly gripping the identity card in his pocket, he strode onto the bridge with all the apparent confidence of Lars Porsena of Clusium on the march to Rome.

The German never even glanced at him.

He bought a railway ticket and travelled to Liège without further incident. There was only one house where he could go, that of Marie-Thérèse's family, and he had no option but to throw himself on their mercy yet again. He walked briskly to the quai Roi Albert, thankful for his friendship with Marie-Thérèse and thankful even for his need of an X-ray that had brought him in touch with the Malaise family.

The house had that blind, withdrawn appearance which told him even before he rang the bell that there was no one there. A chilly little wind picked up the first few autumn leaves and flung them defiantly in Kurt's face. Soon, it would begin to get dark, and with the coming of curfew it would not be safe to walk around the streets.

He had come to the end of the road, and of his luck. He was defeated. There was nowhere else in the world where he could go.

CHAPTER 7

October 1943-September 1944

As Kurt stood there in the street he was joined by another fugitive from Bassines. She was also a friend of Marie-Thérèse coming, as Kurt himself did, to the only shelter she knew. With infectious optimism she expressed her opinion that the Malaise family couldn't be away, and would probably be back at any moment. In order not to attract notice from the neighbours, Kurt hid his suitcase and suggested that they went for a walk while they waited. Half an hour later they returned to find the house as silent as ever.

Having failed to come up with a better alternative, they set out again to quarter the town. This time they walked for well over an hour and Kurt ached all over with the unaccustomed pavement exercise when they arrived once more at the quai Roi Albert. This, they knew, was their last chance. The light was fading; if the Malaises were coming back at all that night, it would have to be in the next few minutes or they would break curfew. If the house were empty this time there was no point in waiting any longer. With darkness and curfew upon them, it was already too late to go anywhere else.

Although there was no light to be seen because of the blackout, there was a different feel about the place this time as they approached it, and presently Marie-Thérèse herself came to the door and greeted them both with affection, and then shocked surprise at their news of the raid on Bassines. She had been to the cinema.

Mme Malaise and her other daughter, Jeanne, who was a student at the hospital, were at home as well, and the three of them agreed to keep the guests for a night or two. The girl who had arrived with Kurt had somewhere else to go the following morning. Kurt, however, with nowhere in the world, had to stay, knowing that his presence imposed an unfair (and dangerous) burden on the family. M Malaise lived and worked in Huy during the week, and when he returned at the weekend he was not best pleased to find Kurt under his roof. If the Germans found out, the whole family would be arrested, with consequences that did not bear thinking. No one could ever be sure of his neighbours; careless talk does not have to be deliberate. Also, here was yet another mouth to feed when getting enough to eat was already a problem.

Kurt was the first to acknowledge the imperative that he should find a safe place to stay on a more permanent basis. The war could go on for a long time yet: the Germans boasted loudly that Europe was an impregnable fortress, while hopes for an Allied landing were still only the vaguest of rumours.

Meanwhile the weather had a sudden final summer fling. Unable to bear the sticky heat any more, Kurt had a wild and desperate urge to go swimming for the first time in literally years. He and the two sisters made their way to the public baths, quite confident that Kurt would be as unrecognisable in the water as he was out of it.

They were wrong. No sooner had he plunged into the green depths than he heard a shriek of joy beside him. Bobbing up, he found himself mobbed by a group of teenagers, descending on him so exuberantly that for a moment he was half afraid they would drown him. Then he recognised them: they were some of the same youngsters who had spent their holidays at Bassines at the time of the crashed bomber. Kurt's delight would have been as great as theirs had it not been for their inevitable greeting. To his utter consternation they all pointed straight at him squealing, 'Look! It's the English spy!'

They had heard what had happened at Bassines and had been particularly worried about their hero. Kurt was out of the water and away almost before the ripples had reached the edge of the pool. Reluctantly, he dared not risk another such confrontation, and the public baths lost their most enthusiastic customer.

The Malaise sisters were tireless in their efforts to find somewhere safe for Kurt to stay, and at one point the family decided that there might be a brief respite for him in the *Hôpital de Bavière*. Jeanne knew one of the registrars who could be trusted, and he agreed to admit Kurt as a patient in the chest department. Liège being a mining town, a large percentage of the patients suffered from chest complaints, so Kurt's presence in the TB ward was unremarkable. He was glad to take the heat off the Malaise family, but he still felt somewhat less than secure in his new hiding place.

Marie-Thérèse visited him every day with reading material and even food, increasing both the risk to herself and Kurt's anxiety. For a start, there was the real danger of catching the disease, not only from the other patients but from eating hospital food – which was anyway appalling. Every other day the consultant came on his rounds, causing endless manipulation on the registrar's part to ensure that he did not stop at Kurt's room to examine him. But there was no escaping the constant attention of a gaggle of medical students, all but one of whom accepted with blind obedience the diagnosis placed before them. The exception was a girl who clearly doubted Kurt's condition, but who was not quite brave enough, mercifully, to question the authority of her superiors.

The nights brought no relief. Patients died with disconcerting frequency; his fear would be heightened by the sound of running footsteps and the inevitable paraphernalia of crisis. Seven floors below, ambulances came and went at all hours, and he would wake to the slamming of car doors and listen panic-stricken in case this time it was the Germans who had discovered he was there, and were even now on their way upstairs to catch him.

The crunch came finally with a routine X-ray for everyone, from which Kurt had been exempted by the registrar. The nurse on duty, however, knew nothing of this, and insisted that it would not hurt him to be done all the same. Kurt, afraid that if he refused too vehemently she would be suspicious, had to submit, and was shepherded along with the other patients, almost hoping that he had managed at last to contract the fell disease. By great good fortune the right registrar was on duty in X-ray that day, and when Kurt arrived he firmly sent him packing. But the incident persuaded him to discharge Kurt forthwith, it being just too difficult and dangerous for both of them to sustain the pretence any longer.

Kurt had to return once more to Marie-Thérèse for lack of anywhere else to go. Ten days of doubtful security (which had felt more like ten weeks) had achieved nothing but a bill from the hospital. Had he left this unpaid it would have been sent eventually to Bonsin, where his identity card had been issued. Then, either he would have become the subject of a great deal more investigation than he dared risk, or else the very people who had acted in his interests would have had to pick up his hospital bill now. He was left with no alternative but to say nothing and settle it himself, although his malingering had cleaned him out of almost every penny he possessed.

He decided that he could not stay on at the quai Roi Albert any longer. The sisters persuaded their father to approach a family friend, a high official in the Liège *gendarmerie*, who seemed to have connections with the Underground. This man offered to find sanctuary for Kurt while his contacts made enquiries for a farm where there was work. There were many of these in isolated spots where it was possible to hide if the Germans came, and which could provide food for an extra labourer. Kurt accepted this suggestion willingly, and although he had to wait while the Underground wheels turned slowly again, the interim period produced for him the unexpected blessing of the start of another greatly valued friendship.

Marie-Thérèse had several young friends in the Girl Guides, among them Eugénie Piette, whose father was a Liège tramway inspector. Kurt took to the father at once: he was a great patriot, a volunteer in the First War who had been one of the first to be wounded. He had been taken to Cambridge with a leg injury, and had fallen in love with England. Now he kept his regimental flag in the loft of his home, and would have defended it with his life against the Germans. His poor little wife was quite different, being scared of everything, and Kurt suspected that her husband's wholehearted and unstinting friendship to people such as himself did nothing to calm her nervous disposition.

Eventually the police officer heard of a safe house in Verviers, one stop beyond Liège on the Aachen line, where Kurt could lodge until a vacancy became available on a farm. It was, of course, a secret destination. On a certain morning, Kurt had to go to the station in Liège, where he was to meet two *gendarmes* who would escort him there. It was unnerving enough to be setting out he knew not where, but that was the least of his anxieties. His identity card, until now such a source of security, suddenly looked more likely to cause his downfall. He had no permission to work in Liège and therefore no reason to be there. Worse, since by German decree everyone had to be employed, those Belgians not working were liable to be sent to Germany. More immediately, there was the constant hazard of a German raid on the station, often heralded by the sudden closing of all the doors, thus cutting off the exit points until everyone's papers had been examined.

Kurt hung around outside the station, reluctant to go in before he must for fear of being caught in a German mousetrap. There were two *gendarmes* by the entrance, but that in itself meant nothing since they always patrolled in pairs. They turned out, however, to be the right ones, and to be as concerned as Kurt himself about the dangers. They had already taken a stroll round the station and had noticed a German officer on the platform who clearly had no intention of travelling.

Five minutes later the same German officer was scrutinising a crowd of passengers waiting for the Verviers train. He glanced at the two *gendarmes* and the young man walking meekly between them, and passed on in search of more suspicious-looking characters. After all, there was nothing more to be said to someone who had already been arrested, and was handcuffed to two *gendarmes* to prove it.

At Verviers, still subject to the uninhibited stares of the other passengers, Kurt consoled himself at the thought of what the same German officer would have done had he been able to watch the three of them trooping into the gents' lavatory strung together like paper dolls, only to emerge singly. In the event, the laugh was nearly on himself as the two *gendarmes* wrestled in a very small space for the better part of ten minutes with a pair of handcuffs which resisted all attempts to unlock them.

He spent about ten days at the safe house. It was a hell with which he had by now grown familiar, but which was no more easily endured for all that. It was run in a totally professional manner by a middle-aged couple who gave him a friendly greeting, asked no questions and put him in the attic. Here he stayed in solitary confinement for the duration of his visit, not out of a preference for his own company but in order not to endanger those who were sheltering him. They brought him adequate supplies of food at suitable intervals, and he would listen to the footsteps coming up the stairs towards him, and also to the sounds of people arriving and departing at the front door, and he would never know whether it was a new lodger or another meal or a German raid upon the house.

Enforced idleness coupled with loneliness greatly exaggerated his now chronic fear, so that he found himself trapped in a whirlpool of depression. To complete his wretchedness he had toothache again, and as this remained untreated without the kindly offices of M Cougnet, an abscess formed. He sat for hour after hour holding a pad soaked in hot water to his face, until eventually the abscess burst. He was lucky: the eruption was external, and as the poison drained away the relief was indescribable, leaving him exhausted, alone, and once more with the trauma of constant anxiety.

At last the two *gendarmes* reappeared with the news that the long-awaited vacancy on a farm had misfired, and there was nothing to be done but for Kurt to return to Liège. He went, very diffidently, to the Piettes' house by the tramway depot, and their response was warm and immediate. Eugénie moved in with her parents and Kurt was given her tiny bedroom, while everything the family could call their own they shared spontaneously with him.

Naturally, Kurt felt he could not allow this situation to last. He continued to agitate for work until another opportunity arose, this time on the Brussels side of Liège, with a safe house at Waremme. Here he stayed with a couple who were respectively a chiropodist and a midwife, and where life was the antithesis of the Verviers attic. The house was in the centre of the town and a great deal too close to the German *Kommandantur* for Kurt's comfort, especially as his host's wireless was permanently tuned to the BBC at full volume, while his conversation was nonstop about the Underground and other subjects much better left unspoken. Kurt was becoming decidedly jumpy after just two days there when the climax came: the chiropodist tried to persuade him to join a hare-brained scheme to inconvenience the Germans by blowing up the railway.

This was too much for Kurt. He was utterly thankful to be transferred to another family, this time consisting of an *inspecteur de ravitaillement*, his wife and their small daughter. The husband's job brought him in contact with all the farms for miles around, an ideal situation for hearing of labouring work.

Everything in this house was on a lavish scale. There was plenty of good food which Kurt soon realised was the result of contact with the inspected farms. Even the dog was an enormous Irish wolfhound, while Madame herself was a voluptuous young woman with a partiality for the sensual pleasures of life. She had a neighbour, cast in the same ample mould, who was a great gossip and would drop in with the latest news during the course of each day. The two ladies would settle down to discuss their not-so-private lives in such uninhibited detail that Kurt felt obliged to absent himself, but they allowed him no such comfort. On the contrary, both were distinctly competitive over the respective merits of their husbands' most intimate statistics, and both called upon Kurt to be the judge of what he heard. It was not only acutely embarrassing, it was positively worse than being lonely. Kurt must have a girlfriend, they protested. But Kurt had no girl-friend, and with a social life that flourished like the Sahara Desert, their conversation made its vast, untracked wastes no easier to bear.

He had been there for less than a week when the neighbour burst in one morning with the news that the Gestapo were in Waremme and had arrested the chiropodist. Kurt did not wait for details: he packed his rucksack and went straight back to Liège, where the Piette family again opened their door to him without hesitation.

They went further than that. M Piette went as far as Marneffe, on a bicycle, to see M Matton. Kurt, who felt him-self to be under considerable moral pressure not to be a bur-den to the Piettes, was thinking that he might seek sanctuary in Marneffe, which was now a prison, and M Piette offered himself as an emissary to find out whether this could be achieved. He was received by M Matton with great cordiality, but returned with the strongest advice to Kurt against such a scheme. Not only did lists of the prisoners' names have to be submitted to the Germans, but Kurt was likely to be recog-nised by many of the wardens who had been recruited from the neighbourhood and would have known him. But quite apart from anything else, M Matton would have no influence to dictate which prison received Kurt, and if he were not sent to Marneffe his predicament would be worse than if he stayed free.

He decided that he would go to Brussels and see his old friend M Watson, arriving at the latter's house one afternoon the following week. Whatever else he had expected, it was not the reception he was given. Mme Watson came hurrying out to him with messages from her husband of the greatest warmth and kindness. But, she insisted, almost pushing Kurt out of the house as she spoke, it was absolutely impossible for him to see anyone just now: he was completely tied up with a very important meeting and Kurt would have to call another day. And with that, he found himself firmly on the pavement.

Altogether, the few days he spent in Brussels proved depressingly fruitless and were laced with bad news. They had started well enough: he found the same owner in the house in the rue Dupont, who was pleased to see him and let him have his old room in the attic. For her safety as well as his own he only stayed there during curfew hours and was out at six o'clock each morning to continue his search for a more permanent hiding place.

Clutching at straws, the only other person who sprang to mind was Herr Winkler. But Herr Winkler's beautiful home was empty. Nobody knew where he was, although apparently he had not been arrested. The owner of the house gave Kurt the address of Herr Winkler's partner, the little clerk who had done business with him – and for him – all the while congratulating himself on his entry into the big time, with the tidy income this provided. Kurt remembered how Herr Winkler had warned the clerk when it would have been wise for him to call a halt, but that the pickings had been too rich for him to quit, and how Herr Winkler had washed his hands and looked the other way.

The clerk's house was in a smart district of Brussels and Kurt was impressed by its magnitude and elegance. The man's wife came to the door and, recognising Kurt, invited him in. The place was sumptuously furnished – albeit lacking the taste of Herr Winkler's flat – and as neat as a museum. Kurt soon discovered the reason for this: the poor girl felt so out of place in these surroundings that she lived almost entirely in the kitchen, although this too was a gleaming palace of modern engineering. Her old father was there and the two children, but her husband was out. With a kind of naive pride, quite devoid of any boastfulness, she told Kurt that he had gone riding. He would not be long if Kurt would care to wait.

When her husband returned he was very short indeed with the visitor. No, he said. He could not help at all.

It was unthinkable, of course, to go to Brussels without looking up the Halberstamms and the Meyerhardts. He found the two doctors just as always, coping well with the ever-deteriorating situation. The next day he set out for the dentist's home in pleasurable anticipation of a chance to explain his sudden and secret departure for Bassines.

But there was no answer. He had expected at least to find Frau Meyerhardt at home, and walked around in search of information. Eventually he managed to raise the owner of the house, and asked her whether the Meyerhardts were out or if there was a new address she could give him. The woman shook her head. Hadn't he heard? The Gestapo had come one day and they had both been arrested.

After that he wandered about aimlessly for a while, as in the old days, his mind numb with pain and disbelief. He came at last to the soup kitchen where he had been accustomed to join with others for a simple meal and to exchange the latest information. There was only one man there whom he remembered, a Roman Catholic priest from one of the nearby churches. They talked for a little, and as Kurt got up to leave the priest told him that if it were any help he would leave the church door unlocked for him. There was a little space, he said, behind the altar where Kurt could hide. As

Kurt thanked him, he added, 'Do you believe in the power of prayer?'

'Yes,' said Kurt.

'I shall pray for you.'

There were about three hours each morning, between the end of curfew and the time when there were people about in the streets again, when Kurt was glad to take advantage of this offer. At considerable risk to himself had he been found out, the priest had not only left the church door unfastened but had left the heating on as well. It was one of the few bright memories in the drabness of that visit.

There was just one other person whom he thought he might contact, a Spanish friend of the Meyerhardts whom he had met once or twice with them. To reach her flat it was necessary to cross the avenue Louise in which were the head-quarters of the Gestapo. Kurt crossed the first carriageway of the wide boulevard as far as the centre, where the tramlines ran between a double avenue of trees. In front of him there was a tram just starting to move, and as Kurt waited for it to pass he glanced up at the windows and happened to catch the eye of one of the passengers. He was a German officer, and he had noticed Kurt – indeed he was staring at him with an interest that was terrifying. There was nothing Kurt could do: he knew he had given himself away by his expression, and if he turned round and went back now, it would be obvious that he was running away. He stood there, rooted to the spot, like a vole that feels the sudden down-rush of air as an owl swoops towards it. The tram was hardly moving; the German officer stood up, still staring at him, and stepped towards the exit. Kurt's legs were jelly, his heart a cold lump somewhere below the belt. There was not a doubt in his mind that this was going to be the end. When the German stepped off the tram Kurt would be picked up, there in the centre of the avenue Louise. He would be taken straight to the cellars of the Gestapo Headquarters and thence to the place of his death.

At that moment the tram accelerated. The German had to sit down and Kurt was left by himself in the middle of the road. The face that had watched him had been arrogant and hostile, cruel even, but it had been in no way remarkable. Nevertheless, because of the hideous threat it represented, its image remained sharply vivid in Kurt's mind. More than fifty years later, of all the nightmares that still haunt him in times of stress, it is the memory of this face staring from the tram window that refuses most obstinately to be laid to rest.

He abandoned his journey, turning back across the road to vanish in the crowd. A few hours later he was on his way to Liège once more. He was desperately unwilling to trespass further on the hospitality of the Piettes, but he was destitute and his confidence was shattered. They received him as before, with open arms.

With Kurt's peace of mind as well as his safety at heart, M Piette set out again for Marneffe. M Matton had been working on the problem meanwhile and sent a message back with him for Kurt, who was to go on a certain day to a café in the *Marché aux Fleurs*, where a Jesuit priest would meet him with further help. Accordingly, Kurt found himself sitting at a table with Fr François who had contacts with the jam factory in Namur, and who thought he could get Kurt a job there if he would like it. It seemed he had been able to do this for others, and among other advantages it would mean that Kurt could live and work officially in Namur. Accepting this offer immediately, Kurt set out in a few days for Namur, where Fr François had promised to meet him at the station and introduce him at the jam factory.

It was a brute of a journey. He spent most of his remaining money on the fare and then waited for two hours on the platform before there was any sign of a train. He boarded the first that was said to be heading in the right direction, only to find that it moved at what seemed little more than a walking pace, stopping at every village on the way and between stations as well, arriving eventually at Namur more than five hours late.

There was no sign of Fr François anywhere. Kurt was in despair; he had not the faintest idea how to proceed. He

walked out into the streets of a strange town where he did not
know a single soul, and without enough money to return to
Liège. The Germans could, and frequently did, make spot
checks on anyone in the street, and Kurt had no right to be in
Namur, nor indeed in Liège, since his identity card was registered in Bonsin. There was no way of finding Fr François,
who very likely operated under a false name anyhow for fear
of German infiltration, and was himself greatly at risk. In
all probability he thought Kurt must have been arrested on
the way, in which case it was even more dangerous for him to
be seen hanging round the station. To add to Kurt's anxiety
and bewilderment, the Germans made constant checks at
every hotel, and there was not very long now before curfew
with all the dangers of being caught homeless on the streets
at nightfall.

After a while he saw a priest and in desperation he crossed
the road to ask him if he knew a Fr François, but the man
shook his head and walked on as if he had not understood the
question. Kurt wandered about for half an hour, fighting to
control a steadily rising panic, and eventually he plucked up
courage to ask a harmless looking passer-by if he knew the
way to the Jesuit Monastery. The man had no idea, but as Kurt
started to walk on, he added that he thought there was a convent somewhere in that direction...

Having no other lead, Kurt walked along the road indicated,
and presently he came to a grey, institutional building with a
suitable inscription over a gothic-style porch. He knocked at
the door and soon a little window opened in it revealing a
nun's face behind a grille. She asked Kurt what he wanted. He
told her simply that he needed help, that he must talk to
someone. Then, as she continued to stand there listening, he
asked her whether by any chance she knew a Jesuit priest
called Fr François, explaining that he had meant to meet him
at the station, but that his train had been five hours late.

His sentence trailed away as the little window was slammed
shut in his face. He waited, because there was nothing else he
could do, although the only sound was the vibration of the
metal grille in his ears. Just as he was about to give up, the

window opened again and the nun reappeared. Her voice was hesitant: clearly she was very frightened. Mother Superior couldn't see him, she said. She didn't know any Fr François, but she suggested that if Kurt went back to the station it was just possible that he might have gone back to look for him there.

He retraced his steps, and there indeed was Fr François waiting at the station. Alas, there was no job to be had at the jam factory after all. Fr François found him a bed for the night and helped him on his way back to Liège next morning, with the consolation that he had other contacts and would get in touch with him again.

A long time later he learned that the convent had been sheltering over a hundred Jewish children.

Fr François did not forget about Kurt. He sent him another message to meet him again at the same café, this time offering him the chance of a job with Englebert, the big rubber manufacturing company at Liège. This part, *Courroies Caoutchouc Industriel*, was in the rue Gretry, and produced conveyor belts for shifting coal at the pitheads. Fr François was in the process of explaining that as neither tyres nor munitions were made there the risk of allied bombing was not great when Kurt's attention was suddenly taken by the sight of a man with his back to them a few tables away. The more Kurt looked at him the more certain he became that it was none other than the chiropodist with a zeal for explosives. A chain of 'ifs' began to link themselves alarmingly in Kurt's mind: if the chiropodist had been freed again after his arrest, it would only have been because of information he could get for the Germans. Moreover, if he wanted to stay free, he would have to make sure that the titbits came in thick and fast. And if Kurt had been seen talking to Fr François, then he did not rate the future chances of either of them very highly. He warned the priest of the possible danger to them both, and they left the café quickly.

A few days later Kurt was summoned for an interview at the factory. He was told he could start the following week after he had obtained a work permit at the local Labour Office. These offices employed Belgians but the system was German, run under German jurisdiction. Kurt thought it quite likely that all the people working there were collaborators. He entered with much trepidation and produced his letter from the factory manager together with his identity card. The girl behind the counter began to fill in an application form for a work permit. It all seemed almost too straightforward.

Half-way through she stopped writing and looked carefully at Kurt's identity card. He leaned forward, as if eager to answer any question she might pose. But she picked up the card and the letter without a glance at him, and took both of them to a little office at the back where a man was sitting at a desk. The door was open and Kurt could see the pair of them conferring, although he could not hear what they said. The two clerks were scrutinising his identity card now, the man indicating something written on it. Kurt found himself breathing as if he had been running a race. Perhaps the girl had recognised his name from some blacklist, or did they already know him as the man who had escaped from Bassines? Or had the chiropodist reported that he had seen him at the café? At any rate, the longer he stayed in the office, the easier he was making it for them to arrest him.

He looked round cautiously. The door was just behind him; he could slip through it and mingle with the people in the street before anyone had missed him. But when they returned with his documents and found that he had run away, they would know he was guilty and the hunt would be on to track him down. The girl was pointing in Kurt's direction now and the man turned a little to get a better view of him. Kurt felt his scalp move, and took half a step towards the street. But no identity card meant no possibility of employment, no food stamps and no right to exist anywhere. Worse still, someone would have to hide and shelter him for as long as the German occupation lasted. He remained where he was by the counter.

The girl was walking towards him now. She handed him back his identity card saying that she couldn't give him the permit that day. He was to come back and fetch it tomorrow. Kurt walked out into the street. He was completely drained, the sweat breaking out all over him. He went into the first café he saw and blew all the rest of his money on a very small brandy.

Later, much shaken by his own reaction to what had happened, he confessed to M Piette that there was no way he could get himself physically through the doors of the Labour Office next morning. His friend's solution was as characteristic as it was practical: he would go for him, of course! Everybody knew him: all he had to do was to say that he was passing and thought he could pick it up for Kurt. 'What could be more natural?' he asked.

He was as good as his word, returning with Kurt's letter from the factory and a permit for him to work there. The problem had been nothing more terrifying than the fact of Kurt's address being stamped at Bonsin while his job was in Liège.

The Malaise sisters and Eugénie Piette rallied round and found him lodgings in the rue Basse-Wez, close to the factory. This was a room on the second floor of a house belonging to a devout Roman Catholic family. They were kind, trustworthy people and the well-furnished room was a great advance on any of the attics he had hitherto occupied, but in no sense could he ever have thought of it as home. He did not mix with the family at all – indeed, he hardly ever saw them unless an air raid brought everyone together in the cellar. Even this was not exactly a social occasion, the only immediate sound being that of the women's low voices interminably saying the rosary.

The son-in-law of the couple who owned the house was extremely pro-German and made no secret of his hostile feelings towards the Allies. Kurt quickly realised that this posed no particular threat to him personally, the man's hatred being centred on Communism and therefore the Russians who at that time were opposing the Nazi regime. These sympathies even gave Kurt a back-handed sense of security: there was very little danger of a German raid on the house, nor any reason to be suspicious about its inhabitants.

But for all this man's bravado when he ranted against the Allies, Kurt was interested to observe his reaction in an air-raid one night when the bombs could be heard much closer than usual. He went entirely to pieces with terror.

The conveyor belts manufactured at the factory where Kurt now worked were made by sticking together layer upon layer of material which was then covered with rubber and vulcanised in huge steam heated presses. The belts were then moved by crane onto a roller, to be put through a smaller mending press. It was Kurt's job, as '*ponceur*', to spot the imperfections and send back for patching any lengths where the rubber was thin enough to show the material. He was harnessed to a two handled sanding machine which smoothed down the overlapping seams of these patches and levelled any uneven lumps that came along. Also, he had to watch out for air pockets in the rubber as these made blisters which had to be sent back for cutting and patching.

It was hard manual labour and unbelievably dirty, as the sanding machine shook him almost senseless, while the appalling dust it raised inevitably found its way into his lungs. The workers were all issued with masks because of this, but as the temperature rose frequently to a punishing 120°F in the steam, it was quite out of the question to wear one. Months later, even at midday in the summer, Kurt shivered coming out into the change of atmosphere, and the night shift was worse still since all the windows had to be kept shut because of the blackout. His colleagues were a rough lot of men, mostly ex-miners and built for manual labour; beside them Kurt felt like a worn-out race-horse harnessed between the shafts of an intolerably heavy cart. He was permanently exhausted in spite of his workers' supplementary milk and allowance of potatoes. Food was terribly scarce: sometimes it was impossible to buy even the meagre rations allotted, and everyone spent long hours queuing for bread which was quite unworthy of the name. This contained a percentage of ground tulip bulbs, and if it were left standing the cut face started to dissolve into a soggy, porridge-like substance.

After a few weeks of this, Kurt's hands developed weeping sores from continuous sweating and contact with the dust particles. The factory doctor diagnosed eczema, a common occupational hazard. His advice was succinct: either it would go or Kurt must.

It went. Other threats to his security soon replaced it. One day a farmer from Marneffe came to look him up and bring messages from M Matton. He described Kurt to one of the girls as she came out of the factory and asked her whether she knew if he were there. The girl had had her eye on Kurt for some weeks and knew exactly whom the stranger meant. Without hesitation, oblivious to possible treachery, she directed him straight to Kurt's lodgings.

Careless talk was not the only kind of danger that lurked in all places at all times. It was impossible to go anywhere in Liège without crossing bridges, all of which were guarded by Germans lying in wait for the unwary. On one occasion Kurt was stopped by two of them when he was on his way to the swimming pool. Having looked at his identity card they demanded to see into the little bag he was carrying, where-upon one of them said to the other, 'Lass ihn gehen'. Forgetting for a moment that he was not supposed to be able to speak any German, Kurt came within an ace of walking on before he had been given permission in French.

To add to the uncertainty, the Germans were not always in uniform. Once when Kurt was walking along the street, a young man just in front of him was approached by a Gestapo officer in plain clothes. Kurt saw the boy waver for a second, then lose his head and start to run. The German suddenly drew a gun and shot him, there in the road, with nothing worse against him than that he had tried to run away. At that moment a car pulled up, the body was bundled in and driven away. The incident was closed; as Kurt forced himself to walk on, the streets were completely empty again. He could almost have wondered whether he had imagined the whole thing.

Fear bred suspicion, and especially of all strangers. A few days after the shooting incident a woman ran up to Kurt in the road, shouting 'Don't go on – there's a German raid in the next street!'

With the memory of the boy's body fresh in his mind, Kurt resisted his first temptation to turn and run away. If this were a trap, his very hesitation would be a give-away; but if not, he was putting his head into a noose by continuing after such a warning. He went on, cautiously. The streets were quiet and empty. He would never know whether a trick had misfired or whether there had indeed been a raid which was all over.

The increased oppression drove him more frequently to seek the company of his friends. Marie-Thérèse visited him often, and he made contact with the Piette family almost daily. Not only was their friendship cheerful and comforting but their little flat was a great deal warmer than Kurt's room, being owned and therefore heated by the tramway company. But in spite of all this kindness he became so run down that he succumbed to a throat infection accompanied by a very high temperature. He managed to buy some tablets containing sulpha drugs over the chemist's counter and, following what he could of the instructions, swallowed a double first dose intended to hit the trouble squarely on the head. The effect was dramatic: the death blow he had dealt the infection very nearly settled all his troubles with the same finality.

Eventually he was well enough to return to work, if not with greater strength, at least with renewed enthusiasm. By now he had discovered the principle of conveyor-belt making. The blisters it was his job to return for patching seemed to have been caused by a failure of the rubber to stick in the first place. Kurt, with time to spare between patches, had the opportunity to walk round and chat to the other workers. As he talked, he handled the rubber going through the process, and very soon he found that he could peel stretches of it off the material surreptitiously, so that by the time it reached his own stage in the work there were many more blisters appearing which had to be returned for re-covering. He hoped that by so doing he was reducing in some small measure the production level of the completed belts, thus adding his own contribution to the sabotage of the German war effort. If questions should be asked about the reason for this suddenly decreased output, he was ready with an answer. By that stage the factory was having to substitute a high proportion of synthetic materials, and no one was in a position to contradict Kurt's theory that the artificial substances did not adhere so well.

Even so, his counter-productive activities were not foolproof. There came a day when he had been talking to a fellow worker and was about to return to his own place. The man glanced at the new blister in the belt before him and remarked casually that now he knew at last what Kurt's job really was.

Kurt was working day-shifts at the time, but for the next three nights he hardly slept at all. At first he decided he would have to go at once – anywhere, as long as there was no trace of him when the Gestapo called at his lodgings. By the next night he was calmer and could debate the risk of staying against the familiar nightmare of losing everything if he ran away. By the third night he was almost sure that if he had been denounced the Germans would have come for him by now, and although he tensed at every sound he heard, he decided to stay.

He was glad enough to stay in the job for the security it gave him, although needless to say in normal circumstances he would never have chosen it. The physical demands of the work in that hellish atmosphere, with its unsocial hours and companions with whom he had so little in common, served to compound his unutterable loneliness. Being uprooted from his background and stripped of his real identity had cut him off not only from the past but from all hope for the future. He drifted aimlessly from one day to the next in a vacuum devoid of any purpose in life beyond survival. Sometimes, returning from the factory late in the evening – for the shift-work necessitated permission to break curfew –

he walked the dead streets in the dark by himself feeling like an alien on some distant planet. Entering his silent lodgings, a stranger even to his empty bed, his body clamoured relentlessly for the warmth of physical contact, the comfort of belonging. At these moments his sense of desolation was complete.

It was true that he had a good friend in Marie-Thérèse, but although the affection they felt for each other was mutual, the relationship never developed beyond this. She belonged to a Roman Catholic family and had had a strict upbringing; Kurt knew that had they become more involved he would never have been considered an acceptable suitor. In the end the unseen barriers of upbringing would have proved insurmountable. Conscious of the inevitable rejection, her presence was a constant reminder that he was missing out on normal life, condemned by enforced isolation to an endless state of celibacy.

At the same time, Kurt recognised his deep dependence on Marie-Thérèse and her friends. Because he did shift work, he often had leisure during the day which he spent in their company, and since personable young men were at a premium during war time, the attraction was mutual. Thus, when three of them turned up one afternoon with the request that he should teach them to play bridge, Kurt was delighted to oblige.

The result was another new friendship. One of the girls, Madeleine Demoulin, shared his love of music, creating a rapport between them. Often on Sundays he would visit her at home with her mother and sister, and they would listen to music on the wireless or even occasionally go to a concert together. Time on his own was usually spent reading. He persuaded the girls to borrow the works of his favourite author for him from the University Library. These books, romantic and lighthearted, often lifted him out of the vicious circle of depression that threatened to overwhelm him. If he read them just before he went to sleep they overcame the nightmare of reality and helped to form the substance of his dreams. By the end of the war he had read every work written by P.G. Wodehouse.

Madeleine was studying to be a social worker, and although he might not have recognised it at the time, perhaps this too struck an answering chord in Kurt. At any rate they found much that they could share, but much also that Kurt felt forced to suppress with the reserve of the perennially persecuted. Madeleine, who was free from these inhibitions, frequently horrified him by the openness of her conversation. True, she told him nothing of the Jews the Demoulins were sheltering in their back room, but she passed on to him cheerfully that one couple she was visiting turned out to have been at Marneffe and had sent him their regards.

To Kurt, the inescapable implication that she had also told them about him had to be regarded as careless talk – just as any kindness from an unknown source had to be treated with suspicion. From time to time he came back from work to find that an envelope containing extra food stamps had been pushed through his door. He was greatly perturbed by this: someone knew where he was hiding. More particularly, his name being on the envelope meant that he was on a list: someone knew that he was on the run. But it was too dangerous to try to sell the stamps on the black market, and he had not enough money to buy the food they represented. Regretfully – for he was very hungry – he decided it was not worth the risk, and he destroyed them.

Many people stood to be endangered if anyone gossiped. The local Underground was immensely active on many fronts of sabotage and subversion, and the Gestapo made prime targets of everyone suspected of being involved with it. The Resistance consisted of small cells working independently of each other for security as well as administration, although there was contact between them. The messengers were usually girls and included Marie-Thérèse's circle of friends. Once, Eugénie Piette had to take a parcel across the town which was large, awkward and heavy. As she climbed onto a tram with it, a German soldier took it and insisted on lifting it for her with a great display of courtesy. Speechless with terror in case he guessed by the feel of it what it contained, Eugénie could only hope that the contents did not part company with the wrapping. All was well, however, and the German never knew that he had gallantly helped the Underground with the transport of a parcel of guns.

Kurt also had charge of something to hide for a few days, which for want of a better place he kept under his bed. His parcel was not as large as Eugénie's had been, and it was softer; he was almost sure that it contained explosives of some sort. Its presence in his room worried him very little until Madeleine came to call. She sat on the bed and innocently lit a cigarette...

Conversation was almost entirely about food: where it had been seen, how to make it go further, the things that people had done to get hold of it. It had become a universal occupation to join any queue in case there was something to eat at the end of it. Everyone went to bed hungry and woke up hungry and dreamed in between of food – good, satisfying food that had simply disappeared. The reality was a monotonous diet of beetroot, cabbage and carrots in various guises, for although almost anything was obtainable on the black market, it was at a price that was prohibitive.

It was not only food, of course, which was in ever shorter supply. Coal was no longer available for domestic use, and at a time when many homes were geared to this kind of fuel only, the hardship in winter was severe. If a coal train was stopped on its journey for some reason, the local children would climb up and grab as much of its load as they could carry. Even the warning shots fired by the Germans into the air did little to deter them, so desperate was the state of siege which prevailed. Kurt spent most of his available winter evenings in the warmth of the Piettes' home, although he dreaded each walk back to his lonely lodgings through the blackout with the spectre of a German on every street corner.

In desperation people resorted to any lengths to enable them to acquire a little extra food. At the factory where Kurt worked the men filched pieces of raw rubber by winding it round themselves under their clothes. Not only could they sell it but there was the added satisfaction of robbing the Germans of a necessary commodity. Kurt did not dare to stick out like a sore thumb by not conforming to this practice: the risk of being taken for a German infiltrator was too great. So he joined the crowd, adding his own share of subversion, although with no intention of running the even greater risk of trying to sell his contraband.

Spring brought its seasonal crop of germs and he fell victim to a heavy cold aggravated by poor diet and unhealthy working conditions. While he shivered and sweated by turns between bouts of coughing, and his eyes and nose ran, it seemed to Kurt that his illness was entirely due to the inevitable shortages. Quite unreasonably, he became obsessed with the notion that if only he could lay hands on a genuine pre-war lemon his recovery would be assured. Without it he was impelled to sneeze his way through to the bitter end, although Mme Piette took pity on him and brought him an even greater prize: a real, fresh egg in a proper shell such as he had not seen in many a long month. It was an unbelievable luxury, and as he well knew a very great sacrifice on the part of the giver.

His physical condition had so deteriorated from malnutrition (which he had suffered two years longer than the Belgians) that the cold took a long time to clear up. As ever, his friends rallied round with practical help. Jeanne Malaise discovered how to obtain biscuits for him on a medical certificate, and these were not only far more palatable than the ghastly *ersatz* bread but much more digestible too, as they contained real flour, which was otherwise quite unobtainable. Gone were the days when the Piettes mixed a paste of it with butter to make the ration go further.

In May the weather improved, and Kurt was just beginning to feel himself again when he was sent for one day at the factory and told to report to someone from Head Office. No reason was given and he had no clue as to what might happen next. He came off the shift with his stomach in a tight, hard knot, his mind racing. When he presented himself, a girl came out to see him. There was some difficulty over his records, she said. They had tried to trace them back to his birth certificate but no one at Ostende had been able to find this. Kurt stared at the papers she had laid before him, his mouth dry, his fingers gripping the counter to steady his hands.

'I think,' he said at last, 'that it must have been destroyed when Ostende was bombed.'

The girl shook her head. That was what they couldn't understand, she said. Apparently it had not been burnt, but no one could find any record of it. Kurt looked dumbly at the letter. There was simply nothing more to be said. There could be only one reason why his records could not be traced, and she was bound to know it.

Suddenly she pointed to where his name was written. They had spelt his name wrong, she said. It was different on his identity card. There must have been a mistake somewhere – she would write back to them. She looked up into his transparent face and Kurt read in her eyes a fleeting glimmer of understanding. She was very busy at the moment, she told him. It would take a long time to get an answer and get it all sorted out.

He relaxed, the life-blood flooding back into his veins. She would see that he was given breathing space. How long, he could not tell, but with a little red tape this sort of enquiry might take months. He walked out into the street, a condemned man reprieved.

Many years afterwards he read that if the war had continued for just six months longer, there would not have been a single Jew left in Europe. Remembering that moment, he knew that this was no exaggeration.

Kurt's suspended sentence did nothing to make him feel safer on the streets, nor indeed elsewhere. For one thing, there was undoubtedly a stronger German presence in the town, with increased policing. More people were being stopped by Germans who were becoming ever more arrogant and harsh in their attitude. Kurt went out as little as possible, but even in his lodgings at night he would lie awake, knowing that any car that stopped, any boots he heard, might mean that the Gestapo had come for him.

But as the increasing fear began to mount, so at the same time a new hope came into being. The Germans were still doggedly pretending that they were winning the war, while their very activity coupled with this accentuated oppression seemed to show that they were in fact jittery. Added to that, propaganda was beginning to penetrate from the other side too. There were whispers of an imminent Allied invasion; at the tramway depot soup-kitchen the grapevine murmured tales of Allied successes and of a turning of the tide.

At the beginning of June Kurt fell ill again, this time with diarrhoea. Having no reserves of health he was by now extremely debilitated, and the problem became so persistent that he had to visit the *Hôpital de Bavière* again, this time as a genuine patient. Here he was given opium to arrest the condition and was told to come back for a second treatment in a few days' time. The date on which he was to return was 6 June 1944.

He arrived to find the hospital seething with an audible buzz of excitement. Someone had heard that the Allies had landed in Normandy and the rumours were spreading like fire through every department. By the time he left the hospital the world outside had changed. The guard on every bridge had been doubled and the already increased German presence was parading, alert and watchful, in every street. Something momentous had happened at last: of that there could now be no doubt. And the reduced volume of German propaganda – indeed, the strange silence of these large numbers of occupying troops – all seemed to point towards the truth of what he had heard.

Kurt went back to work to find the factory alive with the same news. By now it was no longer a rumour: it had been confirmed a certainty. The Allies had invaded.

A suppressed elation rippled through Liège, counterbalanced by a sobering weight of dread. For Kurt, the idea of being caught now, in these last days of the war, was quite unbearable, and the German mood of aggression seemed to make this every day more likely. The Belgians too were as panicky as they were exhilarated: no one could tell what the Germans might do next, and everyone knew that it was not impossible for them all to be deported yet. At the same time, rumours of German defeats and Allied advances abounded. Exactly opposite his lodgings was a small *gendarmerie* in which, to his unceasing amazement, the *gendarme* on duty used to listen to the BBC French service at full blast. The news of Allied victories which wafted across the street to Kurt appeared to corroborate the evidence of his own eyes and ears.

On a couple of occasions there was blanket bombing by the Americans nearby, and although Liège itself was untouched, the area all round the railway bridge over the River Meuse was flattened, leaving only this target intact. Attempts were made to blow up the nearby branch line and tunnel, and at the same time Kurt heard over the policeman's wireless that Paris had fallen. The Allies were sweeping on towards them.

By the beginning of July life in Liège was grinding to a halt. The schools broke up; shops, emptied of all goods, were shutting, and businesses were closing down for an indefinite period. Marie-Thérèse's father came home for the month of August, leaving her much less free to visit Kurt, with the result that he saw more of Madeleine, spending most Sundays with the Demoulins.

Englebert's struggled on for a few weeks longer, finally closing on 2 September. Kurt could not but be thankful to quit the dirt and exhaustion in the intolerable heat of the factory. He lay awake that night in the sultry darkness hearing the restless activity of the Germans in the streets, aware too of the unending drone of aircraft. Presently he got up and went to the window in the hope of finding a breath of cooler air. The noise of planes was louder here – and there was something strange about it.

Then he stiffened, listening intently. The sound he could hear was not aircraft at all; it was heavier, more solid and uneven. The longer he listened the more convinced he became that he could hear the rattling of caterpillar tracks on a road, together with the sound of tanks and lorries changing gear as they started to climb uphill. He wondered briefly whether they were preparing for battle, and then suddenly and forcibly the truth hit him. The house in which he lodged was near the main road to Aachen. If the traffic were climbing, then it was going towards Germany. That could only mean one thing: the Germans were beginning to withdraw.

The following day the Guards Armoured Division liberated Brussels. The capital's radio station was now in Allied hands and the interminable outpouring of German propaganda ceased. The jubilation of everyone in Brussels, at no great distance and yet at that moment in a different world, could be heard on radios which suddenly appeared in every house. Liège fermented with frenzied excitement in a turmoil of emotions. There was overwhelming rejoicing, not unmixed with jealousy for those already liberated, and even tinged with self-pity because Liège was still in German clutches. Stronger than any of these feelings, there was yet another underlying current with which Kurt from long habit found himself identifying: that of stark terror.

Nobody knew what might happen next. The Germans were quite capable of taking reprisals on any number of hostages. There was a hideous precedent for this, fresh in recent memory, when the German Governor Heidrich had been assassinated. An example had been made of this incident: the Czechoslovakian village of Lidice had been razed to the ground and every man, woman and child living there had been killed or deported.

On a more optimistic note, it was also impossible to calculate whether the British or the American armies would break through first. Nevertheless, the gossip on this point of likely military tactics would have led any eavesdropper in the town to suppose that all the inhabitants had become generals overnight. If the British arrived first they would come from the north and the Germans could defend the Meuse, turning Liège into a battlefield. On the other hand, if the Americans came first they would cross the Meuse higher up and could attack the Germans from behind.

In the meantime Kurt had heard quite enough to know that it was time to move out of his distinctly pro-German household. He packed some sensible clothes in his ruck-sack and set out for the Piettes, taking with him the greatest treat he could lay hands on by way of an offering: a tin of sardines.

It was natural enough, he supposed, that everyone who saw him stride out thus equipped should jump to the conclusion that he was on his way to join one of the underground groups. There were many smiles and waves in his direction, and one or two people turned to wish him luck. It was a cheerful walk; Kurt quite enjoyed his assumed glory – until he had to cross the rue de Robermont, the main road leading to the German border. Here he felt rather less than heroic as he contemplated running the gauntlet of a continuous stream of German trucks, each with armed soldiers standing on the running boards, their guns ready. Conscious that if the Belgians had mistaken him for a member of the underground, the Germans could easily do the same, he chose his moment carefully and was thankful to arrive safely at the tramway depot a few minutes later.

His friends as usual pressed him to stay, and the four of them fell to discussing the next move. The rue Frederic Nyst, where the Piettes lived, was on the German side of the River Meuse. If the bridge was held they could find themselves trapped when the Allies arrived. The British held the north of Belgium, but there was no saying from which direction liber-ation would eventually come, and the Meuse could easily prove a positive barrier between themselves and freedom. But it was not so much a question of whether they should cross the river as of whether they were able to do so. Kurt, all too familiar with the sight of redoubled guards on the bridge, came out strongly against an attempt. Having survived so far, his whole being rebelled against taking such a risk at this stage. Mme Piette, nervously making the more cautious choice, sided with him. Eugénie, with the impatience of youth, opted for leaving immediately, while her father, whose opinion Kurt always valued highly, was inclined to think they would probably be wise to try to cross the river while there was any possibility of doing so.

They talked round the problem from all angles. The tramway, like everything else in Liège, had ceased to function. They sat, cooped up in the little flat, discussing every possible eventuality. In the end, as night fell, the only thing they all agreed was that they simply did not know what to do, and would have to wait until next morning.

At that moment there was a series of tremendous bangs and all the lights went out. M Piette sent his terrified little wife to grope for candles and matches, murmuring to Kurt as she left the room that that had settled it for them: no doubt, what they had just heard had been the bridges being blown up. The discussion began again along new lines, with Eugénie suggesting that there might be a boat. This time her father no longer sided with her: they were as safe where they were as anywhere now, he decreed. For the moment they should sit it out and see what happened next.

The following morning M Piette beckoned Kurt quietly to the window and indicated a little group of young men waiting by the trams standing idle in the depot yard. Presently they were joined by two or three more, and the onlookers were horrified to see that these had guns and were quite openly teaching the rest how to use them. They were all, Kurt guessed, scarcely out of their teens, trigger-happy hotheads bent on decisive action regardless of the consequences. And the worst feature of it all was that they were demonstrating their intentions so near to the main road under the ever-watchful eyes of the withdrawing Germans.

Kurt was seized by acute anxiety bordering on panic. If there were a shoot-out in the tramway depot, and an incident of some sort looked more likely every moment, he was trapped as surely as if he were already in a barbed-wire cage. This threat to his life was too cruel; whatever the difficulties he had to get away from this knife edge. He turned abruptly to M Piette and read complete understanding in the older man's face.

Feeling less conspicuous this time, he made his way to the Demoulins' house. He still had to cross the main road, but without his rucksack, for he could hardly arrive with his luggage until he knew that he would be welcome there. Mme Demoulin received him warmly, much relieved at the prospect of having a man about the house at such a time. There remained the problem of fetching his rucksack from the Piettes', crossing and then re-crossing the current of armed Germans yet again. Madeleine volunteered to go with him, a couple being less suspicious than a man on his own. They strolled along, arm-in-arm, trying to appear too intent upon each other's company to heed the departing armies.

The Demoulins lived in the rue Bellevue on the side of a hill overlooking the town. Kurt and Madeleine were able to take a short cut down some steps, thus avoiding most of the traffic, but there could be no ducking out of crossing the rue de Robermont in each direction. On the return journey they were just about to climb the steps leading up to it when a German car appeared behind them, the brakes screeching as it drew level.

It was all so familiar, so inevitable. I have had it, thought Kurt. I have finally run out of lucky breaks. At the end of it all, I am going to be caught now, with freedom almost in sight.

Then the car did a giddy U-turn and shot off down the road again in the opposite direction. As Kurt's breathing returned to normal, the truth dawned. The driver had missed the main road and had found himself suddenly confronted by a foot-path with steps – and a man with a rucksack. Obviously, the Germans had been at least as frightened of Kurt as he of them. The offending rucksack had again caused him to be mistaken for a member of the underground. But now the tables had turned, and to the Germans that had meant that he was an armed man in a dangerous, aggressive mood.

The Demoulin household spent the next two days listening to the wireless, watching from the windows and waiting. From the liberated capital were being broadcast the sounds of victory and celebration; martial music and patriotic songs were interspersed with news of the advancing Allies. But on their own side of the river, to the sound of spasmodic gunfire, the state of siege wore on. There were no shops open and no fresh supplies of anything. They ate as sparingly as possible, conserving what little food remained, not knowing how long it might have to last. Neighbours conferred anxiously as they prepared their cellars against the possibility of further street battles. In the background there was the frequent sound of grenades being lobbed into nearby houses, presumably to flush out any members of the underground who might be hidden there waiting to attack.

Transport for the retreating armies was rapidly running out. The Germans were breaking into premises and commandeering bicycles, most of the remaining Belgian cars having been sabotaged by their owners to prevent them from being of use in the withdrawal. Little groups of pedestrians, mainly *Arbeitsdienst* personnel, could be seen trying desperately to persuade passing vehicles to stop and pick them up, but their pleas fell on deaf ears and they were faced with the prospect of walking back to Germany.

Kurt and his friends watched and waited. Their excitement, though intense, was restrained; it was not all over yet. The Germans were still very much there and anything could happen.

Then, on the morning of Thursday 7 September they woke to see flags in the town. The Americans had arrived in Liège. The whole place gave the impression of a fairground, with every building bedecked overnight and American troops visible in every street. But between these festivities and the road where the Demoulins lived ran the broad barrier of the Meuse. Kurt was, after all, on the wrong side, and could only gaze longingly at freedom from a position which was still fraught with uncertainty.

All that day they watched the celebrations in which they could take no part, and on Friday morning they were still witnessing the last scurryings of the German withdrawal. What had begun as a flood-tide of every kind of vehicle had dwindled to a mere trickle of single trucks and bicycles. Then the flow of even these had begun to dry up, so that eventually the retreat was as spasmodic as a dripping tap. At last the drops became fewer and with longer intervals between each, so that every group of Germans on their stolen bicycles was thought to be the end. The occasional grenade accompanied by the crashing of breaking windows could still be heard, but now a more welcome sound was claiming their attention: rumours that the Americans had crossed further up the river and had finally arrived on their side.

People rushed out with flags, but even as they did so there were hysterical warnings that it was not the Americans after all. In came the flags as another wave of Germans fled along the road, guns raised defiantly, then out with the flags again as word went round that that had surely been the end of them and the Americans would soon be arriving at last. This happened several times until the German retreat was reduced to no more than a few stragglers strung out with great gaps between each. Then there was a long pause; the watchers held their breath; now, surely, the Americans must come.

Suddenly one last cyclist appeared, pedalling for all he was worth towards his native Germany. As he passed, out from behind a building crept another solitary figure, crouched like a cat that stalks a bird. To Kurt's amazement he wore a Belgian army uniform and carried a rifle which he was pointing hopefully in the direction of the retreating German. He must have been a deserter who had managed to stay hidden until it was safe to come out and play the courageous patriot.

After that the rue de Robermont was empty. The silence was complete. Then once more word went round that the Americans were coming; once more the Demoulins and their neighbours hung out the flags of welcome. And this time the shout went up that the Americans had actually been seen on their side of the river. Kurt, with Madeleine and her sister, ran down the slope of the rue Bellevue with all the others to the deserted main road, and presently, unbelievably, like a mirage that turns out to be after all a tangible reality, they saw for themselves American troops, and then a row of tanks progressing slowly towards them.

The men looked appallingly tired, their eyes red-rimmed in their unshaven, haggard faces. It crossed Kurt's mind, even as he stood there cheering and waving with the rest, that it was just as well that the Germans had all gone. These soldiers could not have had an ounce of fight left in them.

At that moment there was a loud explosion, closely followed by another, demonstrating clearly that there must have been after all a few Germans still lurking in the nearby barracks. Kurt and the two girls ran with the crowd to shelter in the nearest building, while the soldiers vanished from the road, throwing themselves down against the cover of the slope. Bits of shrapnel burst all round them, one piece landing a yard from Kurt. Without stopping to think, he put out his hand and took hold of it...

In spite of the pain in his blistered fingers, Kurt's mind was more occupied with curiosity, for the five tanks just stood there in the road making no attempt to respond to the offensive. In another moment the reason for this became clear: the gun turrets opened and out of all of them jumped enough pretty girls to have jammed effectively the turning mechanism of each.

Slowly, the turrets now moved until they pointed towards the source of the attack. The threat was enough: there was no more firing. The guns rotated forwards again and amid the tumult and the shouting the tanks lumbered on along the road.

It was all over. P.G. Wodehouse himself could not have dreamed up a more hilarious climax. Glorious, mad, intoxicating freedom had broken out again at last.

EPILOGUE

After the war Kurt was given the job of starting a children's home at Profonsart, near Brussels, for orphans whose parents had been deported. It was the beginning of a new career for him in social work. Then in May 1947 while on holiday in Wengen, Switzerland, he met Pamela Middleton, an English woman who had a diploma in psychology. They were married in England in September 1948 and have a married son who is a doctor, and three grandchildren.

In 1949 Kurt and Pamela started a children's home in Caversham, about which Pamela has already written in her book, *Children at Treetops*. During this time Kurt took a Diploma of Education at Reading University, and later became a Home Office Inspector for the Children's Department, and then a Social Work Service Officer for the DHSS. He and Pamela still live in Berkshire.

Kurt kept in touch with many of the people he had known during the war, some of whom are still living. Marie-Thérèse, who remains very special to him, married and has three children. She went to live in the Belgian Congo until its independence, and now she lives in Liège again. She and her sister Jeanne, who is an anaesthetist, have both visited the Picks in England and Kurt still corresponds with Marie-Thérèse whom he sees from time to time. He is conscious that he owes her an immense debt of gratitude: not only did she come to his rescue frequently, but it was through her that he met many of his most supportive friends. When Kurt gave her the first draft of his story to read, she devotedly translated the whole book into French for him.

Madeleine Demoulin is married and now lives in London. He saw Mouchie again when he collected his parents' valuables that she had kept for him. She was married and had just given birth to a daughter; after that he lost touch with her. One of these valuables was Frieda Pick's brooch, which Pamela wore on their wedding day.

The Halberstamms survived, although Dr Halberstamm had been arrested on one occasion and beaten up at the Gestapo Headquarters. He was released, however, and after that they had gone into hiding. It was through the Halberstamms that Kurt was given the job of starting the children's home at Profonsart. When Kurt and Pamela were married the Halberstamms gave them a set of solid silver spoons which are much used and greatly treasured in their memory. Dr Halberstamm died soon after the war, his heart never recovering from the strain of the long trek from Marneffe. When their daughter married, Frau Halberstamm went to live with her sister in New York. Kurt received a few letters and then, in spite of writing to her many times, he heard no more, and had to presume that she also had died.

M Matton and M Piette remained the good and loyal friends that they had always been. When Kurt became very ill at the end of 1944, M Piette travelled yet again to Marneffe to tell M Matton that 'Pick was ill'. M Matton fetched Kurt in his car immediately and brought him back to the open prison where he was the Governor. There he fed and nursed Kurt back to health. When Kurt was married, M Matton wrote him two charming letters, but they never met again as M Matton died soon afterwards. M Piette, however, was best man at

Kurt and Pamela's wedding, and Kurt kept up with him and his family for the rest of their lives.

Back in Brussels after the war, one of the first people Kurt tried to contact was M Watson, who had been moved to a high position in the *Ministère de Ravitaillement*. When Kurt ran him to earth he did not at first recognise him. Watson had shaved off his beard when his dealings with the Underground had started to make life dangerous for him. He apologised to Kurt for pushing him out so unceremoniously on the last occasion he had called, explaining that he had had a group of friends in the house at the time. They had discovered that the Gestapo were onto them and were at that very instant frantically deciding whether to go underground. Kurt had arrived at the worst possible moment for himself as well as for them: not even Watson could have been sure that Kurt was not a German plant. M Watson wrote several good recommendations for Kurt to enable him to obtain work, and they corresponded regularly until Watson's letters ceased suddenly.

Another person who reappeared from the Marneffe days was Mandler. He had been arrested once, and though not deported, was taken to the assembly camp at Malines where he had managed to help people with great courage. He turned up at the children's home one Sunday with his wife and son, and thereafter made several visits.

As soon as it was possible to write to Vienna, Kurt got in touch with the Weningers. He learned that they had continued to support his parents for as long as they had remained in Vienna. Frau Weninger used to make constant visits to the grave of a daughter who had died young, and there in the cemetery she would meet Frieda Pick, handing over food and other necessities to her. Kurt heard that they had offered willingly to hide his mother (who did not look at all Jewish) in their home, but of course she would not leave his father. The whole family continued to keep contact with Kurt, and Frau Weninger and her daughter Minnie visited the Picks at their children's home in Caversham.

Herr Spitz, of course, was a survivor. With his Czechoslovakian passport and a baptismal certificate showing him to be a Roman Catholic, he was never registered either as a refugee or as a Jew. Kurt kept up with him for a little, until Herr Spitz's letters stopped arriving.

It goes without saying that Herr Winkler survived, in his beautiful Brussels flat. At the end of the war he was still living well and making money, but whereas everyone else, though penniless, was rejoicing, Herr Winkler was a frightened man. The tables had turned: his business connections, once so remunerative, had landed him on various dangerous lists of racketeers. Nevertheless, he scoffed at Kurt's proposed intention of taking a job running a children's home – for where was the money to be made out of that? Gradually they lost touch, and then one day many years later when Kurt was in Vienna with Pamela and their son, they walked into the Café Mozart, and there, sitting at one of the tables, was Frau Winkler.

His reunion with the professor from Brussels University who had befriended him in 1939 was disappointing. Kurt looked him up at the end of the war and unfortunately, in the course of conversation, referred to the Boche. The professor went off the deep end: he had, it transpired, got away to England, where he had been interned. The Jews in the camp had treated him badly and he was deeply resentful, becoming almost antisemitic in his outlook. His wife begged Kurt to understand but the visitor had taken his leave as quickly as possible, his own feathers more than a little ruffled by the outburst.

Kurt never saw George Kluger again but heard that he had survived. Sadly, he could find out nothing about Herr Schinagl, nor could he discover what had happened to Walter, who had first told him about the job at Marneffe.

There were those whom he knew to have perished. One day, walking in the street, he met the son of the couple who had owned the house in the rue Brogniez, where he had first had a room. Only he and his father were left; his mother and his sister (with whose maths homework Kurt had helped) had been deported.

Herr Winkler's man of business had been less fortunate than his patron. In spite of Herr Winkler's warnings to him, he had continued to cash in on any available racket right up to the arrival of British troops in Brussels. Then, with a brazen lack of tact, he had joined in hanging out the flags. It had been too much for those who knew him. With all their pent up rage and envy boiling over, they had rushed the house, denouncing him as a collaborator. He had lost his head, and rather than face what he knew must be coming to him, he had gone upstairs and shot himself.

In sharp contrast to this sordid little story, Kurt got in touch with Bassines and heard what had become of M Cougnet. When the Gestapo had raided the school, the whole family had been arrested and taken away for questioning. M Cougnet had shouldered full responsibility for the whole organisation and consequently, while his three sons had all survived, M Cougnet himself had perished in a concentration camp. On the wall of the school in Havelange, near Méan, there is a plaque in his honour. It was unveiled on 4 September 1994 in a ceremony marking the fiftieth anniversary of the liberation of Belgium. In the same square is the war memorial commemorating the dead of two world wars. M Cougnet has also been honoured for his steadfast courage by the Israeli Government in Jerusalem at Yad Vashem, the memorial to the victims of the Holocaust.

Enquiries revealed a sad end to the Meyerhardts, too. Frau Meyerhardt had been alone at home when the Gestapo arrived with an order for their arrest. They told her to fetch her husband from his surgery and that they would return in two hours time. In spite of urgent advice from friends that they should disappear immediately, Herr Meyerhardt would not believe that they were in any danger. He was a German who had fought for his country in the first war; he was employed in essential work which would surely exempt him from being deported. Moreover, he believed absolutely that if they co-operated by doing as they were told, such was German justice that no harm could come to them. It was this very patriotism that led to their undoing. Herr Meyerhardt had reckoned entirely without the fact that to the Nazis they no longer counted as Germans. He went home, and together he and his wife waited obediently for the Gestapo to come and arrest them. There was never any news of them again.

Kurt's immediate family numbered 23, of whom by the end of the war 18 had disappeared. These included his closest tie – his parents. He gathered from Herr Weninger that they had been pushed from place to place for some time before being deported on 17 July 1942, via Theresienstadt to the gas chambers of Auschwitz. He could find no further trace of them.

He made exhaustive enquiries through the Red Cross and other international organisations, only to learn that nobody knew what had happened to them, nor did their names appear on any register of those who returned. Finally, he wrote to the police in Vienna. Coming from his own countrymen, their reply was like a slap in the face and left him sick at heart. It seemed that Alfred and Frieda Pick had lived first at this address, then that one and then another. After that, no more was known of them.

They had, the notification said, 'ausgewandert' – 'emigrated'.

Some of the People in the Book

PART I – BRUSSELS

A dentist, his wife and child: a family who lived in the same house as the Picks in Vienna, and who travelled with Kurt to Cologne.

Herr and Frau Sonntag: friends of the above, staying in Brussels.

Herr Schinagl: brother of a friend of the Picks, living in Brussels.

Herr Spitz: an elderly member of Kurt's Viennese rowing club, living in Brussels.

Walter – a young refugee from Vienna to Brussels.

PART II – MARNEFFE AND BRUSSELS

Mandler: a refugee from Vienna, employed as plumber and electrician at the camp.

M Michel Matton: a Belgian prison governor, Director of the camp.

M Verbist, M Bis and a clerical officer, all Belgian civil servants on the staff of the camp.

Madeleine Weil (Mouchie): a teacher from Brussels, employed at the camp.

Obler: an Austrian refugee, working in the camp laundry.

Dr and Frau Halberstamm: refugees from Vienna, both working as GPs at the camp.

Herr and Frau Meyerhardt: a dentist at the camp and his wife, refugees from Berlin.

M Watson: a Belgian inspector of prisons at the *Ministère de la Justice* in Brussels.

M Heckmann: a Belgian financial adviser, stepfather to Mouchie.

Dr Sternberg: a refugee from Vienna, working at the Jewish Committee in Brussels.

PART III — BASSINES AND LIEGE

M Eugéne Cougnet: headmaster, Château de Bassines.

Pierre, André (Puss) and Jean-Jean Cougnet: sons of the above.

Mme van Liefferinge: matron at the school.

Georgie van Liefferinge: son of the above.

George Kluger: a Jewish ex-pupil at the school, working with the above.

Mme Harris (real name: Lore Grunewald): in hiding at the school, pretending to be a nurse.

Marcelle Burette: a teacher at the school from Marchin, near Huy.

Marie-Thérèse Malaise: a teacher at the school from Liège.

Jeanne Malaise: sister of the above, a medical student in Liège.

M and Mme Malaise: parents of the above, living in Liège.

M and Mme Piette: a Liège tramway inspector and his wife.

Eugénie Piette: daughter of the above and a friend of Marie-Thérèse Malaise.

Fr François: a priest from Namur.

Mlle Demoulin: a friend of Marie-Thérèse Malaise, living in Liège.

Mlle Bernaerdt: secretary at the school.

Index

Aachen 3, 11, 12, 13
Albert Canal Fortification 64
Alte Handels Akademie x
Anschluss xi
antisemitism x, xi, 102, 106, 111,
    112, 153, 197
Antwerp 42, 45, 52, 107
Arbeitsdienst 16, 191
Auschwitz 121, 199
Austrian Empire ix
avenue Tervueren, Brussels 115, 116
Avesnes-sur-Helpe xv, 75, 88

Bassines, Château of xiv, 118, 119,
    120, 121, 123, 127-157, 160, 161,
    162
BBC 105, 166, 186
Bernaert, Mlle 141, 157
Bis, M 53, 91, 92, 98
Bohemia ix
Breendonk 116
Brussels 13, 14, 20, 21-48, 52, 65,
    93, 95-121, 168-171
Burette, Marcelle 144

Charleroi 73, 90
Churchill, Winston 105
Ciney 122, 145, 146
Cologne 4, 13
Cougnet, Eugéne 118, 119, 120,
    123, 124, 128-156, 198
Cougnet, Jean-Jean 123, 156, 198
Cougnet, Pierre 127, 128, 131, 133,
    137, 138, 156, 198
Cougnet, 'Puss' 128, 129, 139, 156,
    198
Czechoslovakia ix, 121

Le Panne 97
Demoulin, Madeleine 180, 181, 190,
    192, 193, 195
Dunkirk 97

Emerson, Sir Herbert (later Lord
    Emerson) 62

Englebert, Courroies Caoutchouc
    Industriel 173, 176, 178, 183,
    186
exit stamp 3, 7, 16

feuilles de route 22, 37
Fifth Column 63, 64, 77
François, Fr 171, 172, 173

Gestapo 12, 109, 151, 157, 167, 169,
    177, 181, 198
HQ
    avenue Louise, Brussels 106,
        170, 195
    Hotel Metropole, Morzin Platz,
        Vienna 35
Government, Belgian 22, 52, 54
Guards Armoured Division 187

Halberstamm, Dr and Frau 60, 61,
    67-92, 96, 107, 169, 195
Halifax bomber 132-137, 139
Harris, Mme (Lore Grunewald) 130,
    132, 133
Havelange 123, 198
Heckmann, M 97, 103, 104
Hochschule für Welthandel xi, 38
Hôpital de Bavière 148, 162, 185
Huy 67, 92, 122, 157, 158, 159

International Jewish Joint
    Committee 52, 62

Jewish Refugee Committee 21, 22,
    31, 34, 37, 46, 52, 100, 110, 118,
    120
Judaism 35

Kluger, George 129, 139, 141, 143,
    144, 197
'Koninck, Philippe Georges Kurth'
    148

League of Nations 62
Les Avins-en-Condroz 122
Liège 4, 14, 19, 20, 63, 66, 148, 149,
    160-167, 171-193, 195

Maginot Line 64
Malaise, Jeanne 148, 161, 162, 175, 183, 195
Malaise, Marie-Thérèse xiv, 144, 148, 151, 159, 161, 162, 163, 164, 175, 178, 180, 181, 194, 195
Malines 118, 196
Mandler 53, 57, 58, 62, 70, 71, 196
Maquis 156
Marneffe, Château of xiv, 51-67, 70, 76, 88, 91-93, 98, 99, 116, 167, 168, 171, 195
Matton, Michel 55, 56, 57, 59-67, 70, 97, 98, 116, 167, 171, 195
Meyerhardt, Herr and Frau 60, 67-91, 96, 101, 107, 108, 109, 110, 169, 198, 199
Ministère de la Justice 37, 97, 112, 122, 172
Moravia ix

Namur 67, 90, 171
Neumann's xii
Normandy invasion 185
NSDP (Nazis) xi, xii, xiii, 4, 16, 39, 62, 175, 198
Numerus Clausus x

Obler 57, 58, 116, 117
Ostende 148, 184

Patzau (Pacov) ix
Pick, Alfred ix, 26, 27, 35, 36, 39, 40, 41, 44, 47, 61, 62, 103, 121, 199
Pick, Frieda ix, 26, 27, 36, 39, 61, 62, 121, 195, 196, 199
Pick, Pamela xiii, xiv, 194, 195
Piette, Eugénie 164, 166, 175, 181, 188, 189, 196
Piette, Jules 164, 166, 167, 171, 175, 188, 189, 195, 196
Prague ix
professional smugglers 13-20
Profonsart 194
propaganda, German 88, 105, 110, 185

Real Gymnasium x
Rubinstein 154, 157

rue Brogniez, Brussels 27, 34, 36, 51, 197
rue Dupont, Brussels 95, 109, 119, 120

SA (brown-shirts) 12, 36
Sarma's Stores, Brussels 29, 47
Schey, Baron Friedrich x
Schinagl, Herr 32, 33, 44, 45, 51, 197
Schrebergarten xii
Siegfried Line 8
Sonntag, Herr 21, 23, 25, 38-46
Spitz, Herr 33, 46, 47, 106, 119, 120, 196, 197
SS (black-shirts) 36
Sternberg, Herr and Frau 110, 111

Tabor ix
Theresienstadt 121, 199

Underground Movement
  Belgian 112, 138, 145, 148, 163, 182, 196
  German 63

van Liefferinge, Georgie 129, 137, 139, 140, 151
van Liefferinge, Mme 129, 134
Verbist, M 55, 65, 67, 70
Verviers 164, 165
Vienna ix, xi, xii, 4, 26, 27, 33, 34, 35, 36, 37, 199

war, outbreak of 64
Waremme 166, 167
Watson, M 98, 112, 118, 168, 196
Weil, Madeleine 'Mouchie' 60, 63, 65, 93, 97, 103, 104, 106, 107, 122, 195
Weninger, Frau xii, 196
Weninger, Karl xii, 39, 114, 115, 196, 199
Winkler, Frau 101, 115, 119, 197
Winkler, Herr 95, 96, 101-105, 109, 115, 118, 120, 168, 169, 197
Wodehouse, P.G. 135, 193

Yad Vashem 198
yellow stars 115, 116, 117, 119, 122